IMAGES OF WAR

THE MALAYAN EMERGENCY

THE CRUCIAL YEARS: 1949-53

RARE PHOTOGRAPHS FROM WARTIME ARCHIVES

Mark Forsdike

Pen & Sword
MILITARY

First published in Great Britain in 2022 by
PEN & SWORD MILITARY
an imprint of Pen & Sword Books Ltd
Yorkshire – Philadelphia

Copyright © Mark Forsdike, 2022

ISBN 978-1-39908-224-2

The right of Mark Forsdike to be identified as the author of this work has been asserted by him in accordance with the Copyright, Designs and Patents Act 1988.

A CIP catalogue record for this book is available from the British Library.

All rights reserved. No part of this book may be reproduced or transmitted in any form or by any means, electronic or mechanical including photocopying, recording or by any information storage and retrieval system, without permission from the Publisher in writing.

Typeset by Concept, Huddersfield, West Yorkshire, HD4 5JL.
Printed and bound in England by CPI Group (UK) Ltd, Croydon CR0 4YY.

Pen & Sword Books Limited incorporates the imprints of Atlas, Archaeology, Aviation, Discovery, Family History, Fiction, History, Maritime, Military, Military Classics, Politics, Select, Transport, True Crime, Air World, Frontline Publishing, Leo Cooper, Remember When, Seaforth Publishing, The Praetorian Press, Wharncliffe Local History, Wharncliffe Transport, Wharncliffe True Crime, White Owl and After the Battle.

For a complete list of Pen & Sword titles please contact
PEN & SWORD BOOKS LTD
47 Church Street, Barnsley, South Yorkshire, S70 2AS, England
E-mail: enquiries@pen-and-sword.co.uk
Website: www.pen-and-sword.co.uk
or
PEN & SWORD BOOKS
1950 Lawrence Rd, Havertown, PA 19083, USA
E-mail: uspen-and-sword@casematepublishers.com
Website: www.penandswordbooks.com

Contents

Acknowledgements **5**

Introduction **7**

Author's Notes **9**

Chapter One
Origins of the Emergency **11**

Chapter Two
Acclimatization and Evolution **17**

Chapter Three
The Upper Hand **73**

Chapter Four
'The Best in Their Field' **127**

Chapter Five
The Race for 200 . . . . **191**

Chapter Six
The Fight Continues **243**

Notes **251**

Dedication

To the memory of the twenty-one men of the 1st Suffolk who died on active service during the Malayan Emergency. This work is dedicated in proud and affectionate remembrance of them:

22221729	Sgt. J.A. Ashdown	22329839	Pte. F.L. Lewis
5837855	Sgt. D. Westin	21041416	Pte. R.A. Mills
22305572	Cpl. S. Bailey	22403901	Pte. R. Moore
5883960	Cpl. H. Holland	22078754	Pte. D. Nobbs
21059924	L/Cpl. F.T.C. Mallows	14217245	Pte. L.R. Payne
14459864	L/Cpl. H.R. Simmonds	5774520	Pte. W.G. Pearce
5775902	L/Cpl. S.E. Thompsett	22350436	Pte. E.A. Riches
22614578	Pte. B.V. Ansell	5837859	Bdm. M.S. Swann
22259033	Pte. J.D. Edwards	22444978	Pte. H. Walker
22322782	Pte. L.G. Killick	22395548	Pte. D. Wilson
22602535	Pte. B. Larman		

Acknowledgements

It has taken a long time for this book to come to fruition, but it would not have been possible without the much appreciated assistance of the numerous veterans of the Suffolk Regiment who generously gave their time to be interviewed and allowed their photographs to be copied for inclusion in this work.

This project started many years ago, and sadly the large majority of those whose reminiscences follow have now passed away. Special thanks must go to the following veterans of the regiment: Ken Ambrose, Dave Arthur, Richard Baldwin, John Blench, Sid Brace, Gordon Broughton, Ray Burwood, John Bye, Tony Cobbold, Tony Coote, Bill Deller, Hugh Doran, Maurice Etienne, George Flory, Adrian Gillmore, Ernie Guest, Ray Hands, Alan Horrex, Jim Hurst, John Hopkins, Pat Hopper, Sonny Horton, Fred Key, Alex Knightly, 'Fuzzy' Knights, Denis Leavitt, Patrick Macdonald, Dick May, Fred Mullinder, Ron Newlands, Ron Norton, 'Pedlar' Palmer, Michael Pickard, Bernie Phillips, Don Randall, Richard Scott, Peter Todd and Richard Wilson.

Special mention should be made of the late Tony Rogers from the Hemel Hempstead Branch of the Suffolk Regiment Old Comrades Association for the continual supply of photographs of the regiment that he sent me and for the contact details of many a Suffolk Malaya veteran which resulted in my travelling the length and breadth of the country to conduct interviews.

I am also exceedingly grateful to my good friend Taff Gillingham for introducing me to many members of the battalion back in 2001 at one of their annual BBQs; an event that started my interest in the campaign and which has ultimately resulted in this book. He has also been most generous in allowing me to include photographs from the album of Sergeant Aldridge in the book.

My special thanks go to National Service subalterns Pat Bird and Martin Knowles who, along with the late Robin Farmer, were known affectionately in Malaya as the 'Three Musketeers'. All were most generous with their time and in answering the numerous questions I asked of them. For a young historian, worried about asking daunting questions of former Suffolk Regiment officers, they were all most kind and helpful to me, for which I am most grateful.

I am also grateful to my wife Emma, and to my children Lily and George, for all their ongoing support and understanding during the compilation of the book.

My most sincere thanks must go to Len Spicer, who has been a most helpful guide to me during the collation of this book. Len's own book *The Suffolks in Malaya* (Lawson Phelps, 1998) is still the most detailed work on the Battalion's part in the Emergency. He has been most supportive to me in this project and has been a supreme knowledge base for all the unusual questions that I have asked of him over the years.

Finally, of all the veterans of the battalion that I interviewed one man stands out, and that was Bernard Elmer. To me 'Bernie' was the epitome of the fighting Suffolk soldier. He had a wry sense of humour and never suffered fools gladly. He was one of the very first veterans that I interviewed and I returned numerous times to see him and his wife Margaret before he sadly died in 2012. He told me many tales of his army life and of the people with whom he served. Always happy to see me, he never glorified nor embellished his actions and recounted many a fascinating tale of his sometimes funny, sometimes frightening, service in Malaya. As with all those Suffolk veterans I have had the honour to meet, he was a true gentleman.

Introduction

Throughout the late 1990s and early 2000s, the veterans of the Malayan Emergency dominated Suffolk Regimental gatherings. Despite the men of the wartime generations becoming fewer in number on parade, there seemed to be an ever-increasing number of men who had served in Malaya attending reunions. This was in no small way due to the actions of Tony Rogers and Ray Burdett, who together embarked on a campaign to track down as many men of their old battalion who served in Malaya as could be found and bring them to Bury St Edmunds for the annual regimental gathering held each August.

Unlike many of their contemporaries, they embraced the internet and were successful in finding former Suffolk soldiers all across the world, which they enrolled as members of the Hemel Hempstead Branch of the Old Comrades Association. Within a year, its membership had risen from fewer than 20 to more than 200 members, making it the largest branch of the association ever to exist.

In parallel to their efforts, another Suffolk veteran, John Blench, held a free annual BBQ for all veterans of the Malayan Emergency on his farm near Peterborough. His generosity ensured that for many years there was an annual event just for veterans of that campaign and this without doubt helped to maintain the close bonds that these men had with one another.

The men who congregated at these events – usually with a beer in hand – relived campaigns in the jungle and fights with terrorists, but they never forgot their comrades who were killed in action. They were all most keen to accept me into their 'ranks' as someone who was eager to know more of their service in far-off Malaya, and all were pleased to share their stories and photographs with someone who took an interest in their military service of more than fifty years earlier.

The majority of those that I met felt that the Malayan Emergency was very much a 'forgotten war' overshadowed by other post-war conflicts, but all felt keenly that the part they played in it should not be forgotten.

What interested me most about this campaign was the large number of photographs that survived from it. Compared to previous wars and engagements, Malaya seemed to be the first conflict of the private camera for the men of the Suffolk Regiment and many a young National Serviceman who had never been away from home before took a good many photographs of his time abroad, chiefly as a souvenir of his service in far-off places to which he could never afford to return.

Those photographs, some of which have been brought together here for the first time, show a cross-section of a battalion operating at the height of the Emergency. They show the rigours of a campaign that at times pushed men to the limits of physical and mental endurance, but also gave those same young men the first real independence they had felt in their lives. The campaign in Malaya fostered a special form of regimental comradeship, which still survives to this day.

Now, seventy years on from their service, I hope that this book will go some way to ensuring that, as many Suffolk veterans wished, their service in Malaya should not be forgotten, and for the surviving veterans of the battalion and the descendants of those who are sadly no longer with us, that it will help keep alive the proud memory of what the Suffolk Regiment achieved in Malaya all those years ago.

Mark Forsdike
2021

Author's Note

Every possible effort has been made to reproduce the highest quality of images in this volume. The reader should, however, bear in mind that the vast majority of the photographs seen in this book were taken on small compact 'Brownie'-style cameras, and were usually printed no larger than 2 × 2 inches. Many were taken hastily and in extremes of lighting – either in harsh sunlight or in the dark confines of the jungle – so there will be a certain amount of variance in brightness and contrast.

Every possible effort has also been made to check and to confirm the names of those captured on the following pages, and the places where the original photographs were taken. The vast majority of the information has been supplied by the veterans themselves, but with the passing of time, mistakes of memory do occur and the author would be pleased to receive any corrections should a reader spot an error.

Throughout this book, you will see the term 'bandits' being used. This term was used by both the Japanese and Chiang Kai-shek during the war to describe 'communists'. In an effort to distance themselves from this in the eyes of the Malayan Chinese communities, the British changed their official phraseology to 'communist terrorist' or 'CT' for short. However, every veteran I spoke with always referred to them as 'bandits' and so this term has been used in the text that follows.

Readers should also be aware of the graphic nature of some of the images, particularly those of dead terrorists. A minimal number of such images have been included here for context in the overall story of the campaign.

Chapter One

Origins of the Emergency

In the final analysis, success or failure after months, even years of wearisome patrolling, depended almost entirely on the split-second reaction of a young National Serviceman, and in his case, Hands was the name, and when Hands' father was told that he'd won the Military Cross, he said 'I am surprised, I thought my son was rather a bookworm.' Parents never do know, do they.[1]

[Sir Brian Horrocks speaking of an action of the Suffolk Regiment during the Malayan Emergency.]

In 1948 the world was still very much in turmoil. The British were fighting a difficult battle on many fronts from the myriad of Empire nations that now wished to be free from their rule. India gained its independence in August 1947, and ten months later the British Mandate in Palestine finally ended. In the east, Malaya was to be the next colony, thrown into a prolonged insurgent war in which a small, elusive communist enemy would wage havoc and fear on its people for more than a decade in their attempt to end British rule.

At that time Malaya was Britain's richest colony, responsible for meeting more than half the world's demand for natural rubber. In an age before synthetics, this was a valuable commodity. In addition to this, the country also supplied more than a third of the world's tin and had large natural reserves of coal, together with large forests of timber, badly needed at home for post-war rebuilding.

However, with fluctuating demand for such commodities, the Malayan economy was very much in a 'boom or bust' situation. Many of the native Malays were forced out of work by the immigrant Chinese who took their jobs in the mines and forced them to work on the rubber plantations that could be subject to 'feast or famine' working conditions. As a consequence of this, tensions heightened between Malaya's many races, which also included Indians and Europeans.

Attempts by Britain to create the 'Malay Union' in 1946 to give equal rights to all citizens were rejected by the Malays in many of the states under British control and in 1948 the Union was abolished and the 'Federation of Malaya' was created.

The Federation consisted of eleven separate states bound together under British administration. Of these, nine states were Malay, with only two being British (Malacca

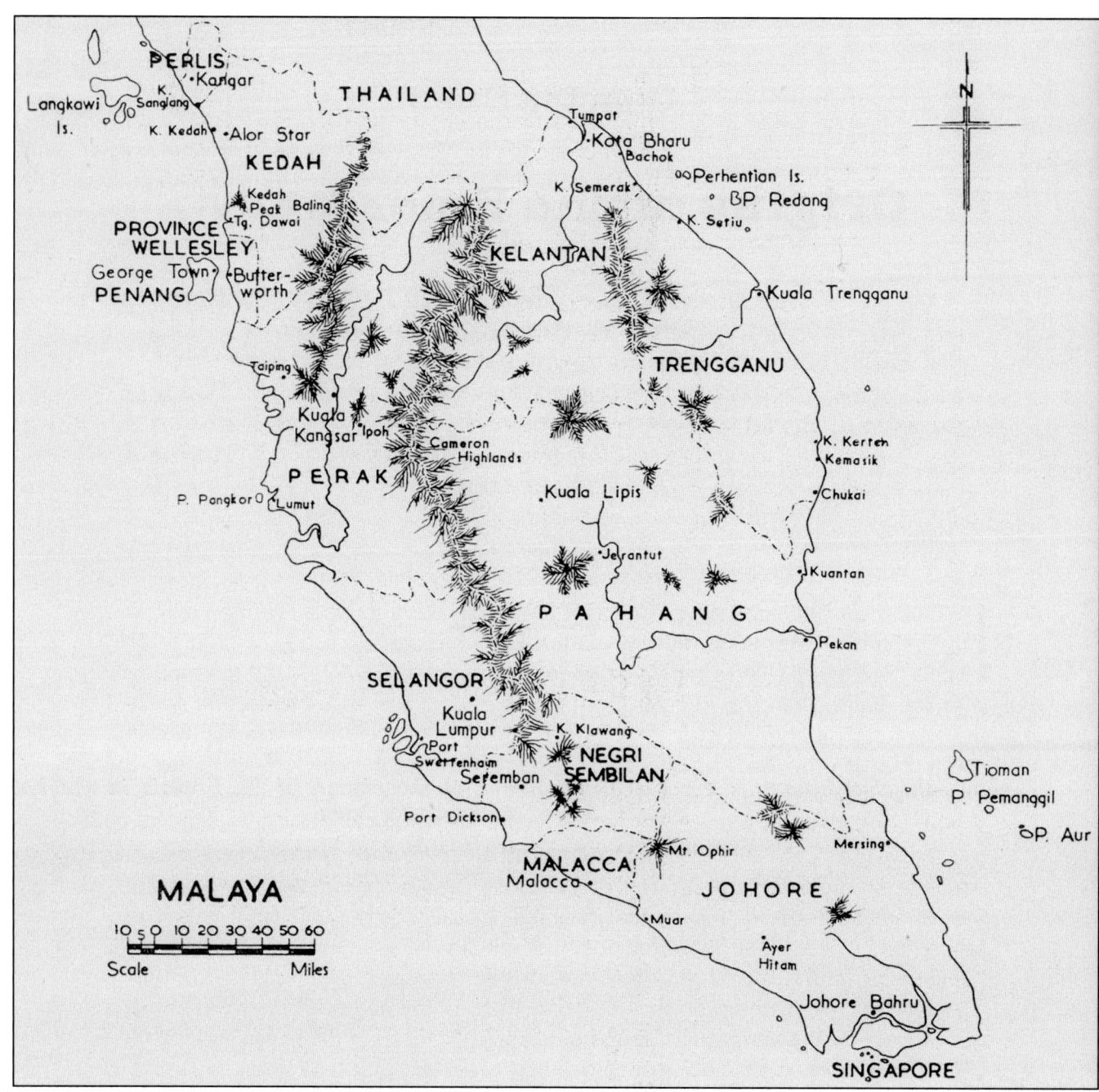

The colony of Malaya.

and Penang). It was headed by a high commissioner responsible for all civil, judicial and administrative affairs. It sought to reduce Chinese influence in the colony, but frustrated the Chinese who saw these actions as a betrayal, especially since during Malaya's wartime occupation it was they who had suffered most under the brutal Japanese regime.

With an ever-growing trade union movement flourishing in the Chinese communities and increased support for the Chinese cause coming from the Malayan Communist Party which had been in existence for almost twenty years, by 1948 a group of young Chinese communists sought to make a difference and aimed to establish 'liberated' areas within Malaya that would be free of British control and where their ideal of communism could spread.

To achieve this, fear and violence were to be their weapons, and soon they would fire the opening shots against the colonial administration in what was to become a twelve-year conflict that brought Britain sharply into the Cold War.

On 16 June 1948 in Perak on the west coast of Malaya, Chinese terrorists killed three European planters. Two days later, the Federation enacted special emergency measures to counteract such occurrences happening again. Two weeks later, these measures came into force banning many trade unions and the Malayan Communist Party. The Federation Police were now given special powers to detain suspected communists and those suspected of assisting them in acts of terrorism, but in a country where almost half the population were Chinese, distinguishing friend from foe was going to prove to be a difficult task.

Naturally relations between the Federation's civil powers and the local Chinese populations began to break down, and in secret, support for the communist cause was growing fast among the immigrant Chinese population. Soon an undercover organization, the MRLA (Malay Races Liberation Army) was formed with the purpose of waging war against British rule and bringing about the eventual independence of Malaya as a communist state.

The backbone of the new organization was rooted in a wartime force known as the MPAJA (Malayan People's Anti-Japanese Army). This had been a predominantly communist force that had fought undercover in the jungles of Malaya against the Japanese. During the war years, these men and women were fighters loyal to the Allied cause and their political allegiances were forgotten as the Allies armed them to fight alongside their own clandestine units in the jungle.

Upon disbandment in late 1945, many refused to surrender their weapons and went into hiding. Many more hid their weapons in jungle caches ready for potential future use. Those MPAJA troops in public now openly sported the red star badge of the communists. Former comrades had now become enemies.

Concerned by the huge insurance premiums that would undoubtedly have to be paid should a state of war be declared, the Federation instead enacted a state of emergency and asked for support from Great Britain's armed forces to assist the civil powers in containing and eliminating the threat of a potential communist takeover. Martial law, however, was never resorted to during the Emergency.

In a country that was then four-fifths covered in jungle, initial hesitant progress was made in defeating the terrorists. The fight would have to be taken to them in their jungle bases and the security forces would soon learn from their initial mistakes. In the years that followed, the civil powers, in close co-operation with the armed forces, set about breaking down the communist network through various methods of intelligence-gathering and each valuable lead was rigorously followed up, often resulting in the elimination or capture of 'bandits' in the targeted area.

Later the Chinese squatters – the crucial link between the terrorists in the jungle and their supplies of arms and food – were removed and rehoused, forcing the terrorists deeper into the jungle, where they would be compelled to remain until long-range patrols could venture out to hunt for them, normally using helicopters to land at locations in minutes that would have previously taken days of arduous trekking to reach.

Though the Emergency was to linger on past Malayan independence in 1957, it was in the first five years that the decisive blow to defeat the terrorists was dealt.

Throughout the Emergency, numerous British and Commonwealth units served in Malaya, usually for around two years' duration with varying success in the areas in which they were deployed. However, one unit stands out as the exception, being the most successful British infantry battalion to serve during the Emergency: the 1st Battalion, the Suffolk Regiment.

During their service in Malaya, 1st Suffolk waged a progressive and active campaign against the terrorists, resulting in the dissipation of bandit forces around the town of Kajang and across the capital state of Selangor. By the end of their tour, which was extended due to their continued success, they had notched up an impressive record of 'bandits' killed and captured; a record that was never surpassed by any other British unit serving during the Emergency.

This book tells the story of that battalion and its service in Malaya between August 1949 and January 1953 in what have since been described as the 'crucial' years.

It was often cited later that the battalion owed its success to its men coming from a rural area, but in fact almost 50 per cent of the men who served within its ranks in Malaya came not from Suffolk but from the north London suburbs and from Hertfordshire. Such were their proportions in its ranks that at one time the battalion was nicknamed 'the Dagenham Light Infantry'.

It was, however, the zeal and tenacity of these young men, the majority of whom were conscripted National Servicemen, to close with the enemy and to hunt them out at all costs that led to their success. The battalion exploited the skills of native trackers and learned much from them. They worked in the closest co-operation with the police and security forces, acting swiftly upon information received. Swiftness was often the key to their success.

In a volume such as this it is not possible to record the day-to-day activities of the battalion or to chart the Emergency blow by blow, but this book, it is hoped, will show the history of an operational battalion that adapted well to its surroundings and achieved outstanding results by its dedication to the task it was required to perform. This was made possible by the close-knit family community of the regiment and the spirit it fostered of fierce rivalry between platoons to be the best at their job, which was by its nature a very callous business.

This is a Suffolk Regiment story, but it could be said that it was the same story for any number of Commonwealth units serving in Malaya, each adapting in their own way to their surroundings and to the overall requirement to defeat a ruthless, unorthodox and largely unseen enemy.

Detail of the Suffolk Regiment's primary area of operations in the state of Selangor.

Chapter Two

Acclimatization and Evolution

On 1 July 1949, the troopship *Dilwara* docked at Singapore. It brought troops from numerous postings in the Mediterranean and Middle East including the Suffolk Regiment which had just finished a tour of duty in Greece.

The 1st Battalion, which was by then the only regular battalion of the regiment, was woefully under strength. In its last few weeks before it left Greece, a thorough reorganization had taken place. Operation 'Sort Out' had seen large numbers of men transferred to the Bedfordshire and Hertfordshire Regiment and vice versa. All men had to be fit for the next posting of the regiment, and even during the journey this 'weeding out' process continued.

Upon arrival at Singapore, the battalion spent a fortnight at the Nee Soon camp where it started training for service in the jungle. Although everybody was fit and new drafts of younger men had joined them on the journey, the battalion was still well below operational strength. At that time it comprised just 28 officers and 520 other ranks compared to a wartime complement of around 850 all ranks.

After a brief few days, the battalion entrained for Selangor state in Malaya. The journey up country was long and hot. The train moved slowly, but the terrorists had already made several daring attacks on locomotives in the previous weeks and on Malaya's single-track railway lines a halt in the jungle might result in a costly ambush.

The journey of 215 miles was uneventful, with the battalion arriving the following morning. In their new positions, training continued in earnest. The battalion was now to form part of the 2nd Guards Brigade and would eventually take over operational commitments from the 3rd Battalion, Grenadier Guards.

Throughout their time in Malaya, Selangor was to be their main base of operations. For the next three and a half years, patrols would be launched from here and from other smaller outstations.

Their new base was Wardieburn Camp at Sungei Besi, about 3 miles south of the Malayan capital Kuala Lumpur. Accommodation was of differing styles with the mess halls and kitchens being 'Indian-pattern' huts of attap leaf panels on a steel frame. The stores, offices and MT shed were of the traditional Nissen hut style. Some company accommodation was tented, with the canvas being slung over steel frames. This was arranged to the south side of the camp in blocks with roadways in between.

In those early days the battalion learned much from their neighbours, the 2nd Battalion, Scots Guards, with whom they were sharing the camp. Daily they gave lectures, and every afternoon the battalion went out in company blocks to the nearby firing range to learn jungle tactics and to train on various weapons such as flame-throwers and anti-tank guns. In reality, neither of these weapons would serve any useful purpose in the conflict that was to come.

In early August, a draft of 9 NCOs and 136 other ranks arrived earlier than anticipated and in an intense two weeks they joined the rifle companies in training. The majority of men in this draft were National Servicemen: young 19-year-olds who would spend the next eighteen months with the battalion. Some had been evacuated during the war, but many had never before left their home towns or villages.

'Sonny' or 'Tiger' Horton was a young National Serviceman from Great Yarmouth. He remembered the 'adventure':

> I'd never been abroad, not even a day trip to France, so it was quite a thing to be called up, and having to travel to Colchester. Within a few weeks, I was sailing the world. It was all great 'til we hit Malaya, then the fun started, though I shouldn't complain; a friend of mine was called up not long after me and he ended up going to Korea.[1]

Within days, the battalion was thrown into active operations in support of the civil powers. Their first 'proper' patrol began on 20 August when 'D' Company moved off to officially take over positions from the Scots Guards.

The battalion drew its first blood on 24 August when a patrol of 10 Platoon, 'D' Company under the command of Second Lieutenant Starling made the first successful contact with the enemy between the Cheras Road and Kampong Sungei Long.

They had been checking a section of water pipeline when they spotted a track into the jungle. Following it cautiously, they soon came to a small clearing where, unaware that they were being watched, a party of ten bandits was in conference. Opening fire, two were killed, with a third badly wounded who later died. The remainder fled into the undergrowth. A haul of weapons and packs was recovered that confirmed the bandits had been part of the notorious 'Kajang Gang' led by the bearded bandit leader Liew Kon Kim. He was to be the nemesis of the battalion for the next two and a half years.

The following day a patrol working in co-operation with the Federation Police surprised a party of bandits trying to sabotage rubber trees on the Sidney Estate in Broga. Two were killed, but others fled. 'A' Company met with lesser success the following day when a patrol met eight bandits but failed to get any of them, but within a fortnight of commencing active operations, the battalion had accounted for eight bandits killed. They had made a good start.

Another success came in late September 1949 with Operation LOWESTOFT. An informant, who had previously given good reliable information, told the police that a party of bandits would be emerging from the jungle at a spot south of Broga on the afternoon of 23 September.

Organizing an operation along the lines of the Lowestoft fishing fleet (hence its name), the battalion planned a two-pronged attack. 'C' Company under the command of Major Devey would act in the role of the 'Trawlers' and would sweep the jungle to push the bandits to a stop line where 'D' Company would be waiting for them.

For the plan to work, complete secrecy was necessary. 'C' Company would travel in civilian trucks right up to the edge of the jungle before debussing. 'D' Company would take a long and winding approach to their stop line as a ruse to ensure that anyone reporting their movements to the bandits would be confused as to their final destination. To guard against any form of mistaken identity, 'C' Company wore white bandages around their jungle hats.

As 'C' Company waited, a party of bandits made their move towards 'D' Company's stop line. Just after 2.00pm, 'D' Company opened fire on three bandits who were making a break to the north-west corner of 'C' Company's area. Fire was exchanged and one bandit was killed, with the others going to ground in the undergrowth.

The intelligence officer now used the commanding officer's scout car which was armed with twin Vickers 'K' guns to rake the ground. Waiting patiently, fifteen minutes later a fire was reported at a nearby bungalow where a second group of bandits was trying to break out of the jungle. They were caught by a section led by Second Lieutenant Jimmy Kelly, who fired at one bandit while running after him. He brought him down with fire from his carbine at a distance of about 100 yards. His section's Bren-gunner beside him accounted for another two.

Now with the archaic sound of a bugle – which carried far above the buzzing of jungle life – 'C' Company started their sweep and reached the road an hour later. No more bandits were found, but Major Devey was aware that at least three more were still known to be in the area and he started to sweep back the way they had come.

Moving silently back, Corporal 'Nanny' Keeble stalked his previous track. Then in the undergrowth to his right, he heard the familiar sound of a Sten gun being cocked. Immediately he threw a phosphorous grenade in that direction and one bandit stood up to surrender. His colleague, who bolted for the jungle, was brought down by rifle fire from one of Keeble's comrades.

Further along the track, another bandit emerged from hiding and fired back at 'C' Company. Corporal Ron Evans was, however, quicker off the mark and brought him down. The action resulted in four bandits being killed and three captured, along with several weapons, packs and ammunition.

The use of bandages as a tactical recognition sign was noted to be necessary, but it was realized that white looked, at a quick glance, to be like the material of a bandit's khaki drill shirt. It was proposed that the men should wear 'Minden Roses' in their hats 'in accordance with the best traditions of the regiment'[2] but this was not a practical alternative for small red and yellow roses would be virtually indistinguishable in the dark interior of the jungle.

Roses were worn every year in honour of the regiment's principal battle honour of 1759 when it was said that roses were plucked by the men of the regiment as they went into battle. The Suffolk Regiment carried as its arms the Castle and Key of Gibraltar in recognition of their participation in the Great Siege of 1779–83 and instead of roses, yellow dusters were cut up to fashion into castles that were instead sewn onto the front of their jungle hats.

This was the first time that the need for total secrecy in such operations became apparent, together with thorough co-operation between the battalion and the local police. In these initial operations success varied as the battalion found its feet and in those early days a strict rota of operations was kept up; five days out, with two days in. Soon all realized that to eliminate the terrorists, the battalion would need to be more flexible and would need to be ready to operate twenty-four hours a day, seven days a week. The battalion commander, Lieutenant Colonel Ian Wight, therefore created a rota of 'standby platoons' that could be kept in camp ready to move at ten minutes' notice if needed.

The rigidity and inflexibility of those early routines, coupled with the inevitable 'learning on the job', soon became all too apparent, for within a week of these successes the battalion lost three of its members on active service. Lance Corporal Edwards was killed on a 'D' Company patrol on 19 September and a week later Privates Payne and Nobbs were killed when their patrol of 'A' Company was ambushed near Broga.

It was clear that this was no ordinary enemy and here in the jungle, there were no front lines. The men soon lost any illusions that this posting was going to be 'cushy' and realized that it would be a deadly and long-drawn-out game of 'hide and seek' in the shadows of the jungle.

In late September, another patrol led by Second Lieutenant Starling met with yet more success. They had been out some miles from camp when just before midday they came across a small hill in the jungle and were fired upon by a party of bandits. Without a thought for himself, Starling shouted 'Charge!' and led his patrol forward in pursuit. Running up the hill, he successfully routed the bandits by firing his Sten gun from the hip. The bandits fled, leaving everything except their weapons.

Seeing them fleeing along a track away from the summit on the other side, Starling continued in pursuit with his patrol following. About half a mile on, they came across an abandoned bandit camp, but further along the track another hilltop camp was spotted with bandits furiously packing up their equipment. This second camp was only accessible via a steep staircase.

Approaching it, Starling rushed up the steps, firing at the bandits on the summit. They returned fire and one armed with an old Sten gun shot back, wounding Starling twice in the face. By a miracle the bandit's ammunition was old and defective, leaving Starling with only a grazed lip and temple.

Shouting back to his sergeant that he'd been hit, Starling still charged on, following another bandit down the steep slopes on the other side and away into the undergrowth. Despite a spirited chase, the patrol was forced to abandon their pursuit. One man had been wounded in the action and was now bleeding heavily. Unable to make radio contact with base, Starling now left his sergeant in charge of the patrol and set off to get urgent help for the wounded man.

For more than two hours he ran before reaching a planter's bungalow from where, exhausted, he telephoned the police, who passed a message back to the battalion. Starling immediately returned to collect his men and lead them back to their collection point. In his absence, the wounded man had been conveyed to a homemade stretcher and his wounds had been dressed, but he was now unconscious. By the time they got back into camp, the patrol had been out for more than fifteen hours. Only after the wounded man was taken to hospital and he was sure that all his men were well did Starling go for medical aid for his own wounds.

For his actions that day 'Joe' Starling was awarded the Military Cross. His wound was painful and in an effort to allow the skin to heal across his upper lip, the medical officer suggested that he should grow a moustache, which he did. The battalion commander Lieutenant Colonel Ian Wight wrote later of the action:

> A combination of quick reaction and the offensive spirit routed the enemy. The effect of this on the rest of the Battalion was electric and in no time at all men had convinced themselves they were better fighters than the enemy, and although we did have setbacks, they were far exceeded by our successes.[3]

The euphoria of the award of the first Military Cross of the campaign was bitterly tempered by the harsh realities of dealing with such an enemy. Bandsman Michael 'Mickey' Swann later died of his wounds. Boy Swann had joined the battalion in Palestine in 1945 aged 14 before being sent to the Royal Military School of Music at Kneller Hall. He had only been ordered out on patrol that day because of a shortage of available men. Such was the ill feeling within the band and drums that a permanent stop was placed on using its members on operations.

The battalion had seen many changes in their first six months of service in Malaya, not only in their ethos and tactics but also in their arms and equipment. By early 1950 the men were learning to adapt not only themselves but also their kit to the rigours of the campaign.

The original arrivals from Greece wore scrubbed wartime webbing that showed in brilliant contrast to the new jungle green uniforms they were issued. On their feet, they patrolled originally in hobnailed 'ammunition' boots and gaiters, which were quite unsuitable for the muddy, slippery terrain. They were replaced pretty rapidly with a pair of more comfortable and practical canvas and rubber jungle boots.

Copied from American wartime designs, these boots were laced up, with hooks at the top. Reinforced at the ankles with rubber patches, these were often removed as they would squeak with amazing loudness when on watch in the dead of night. By January 1953, at the end of their tour, it was stated that the battalion had worn out 15,000 pairs of them, an average of 6 pairs per man.

In early 1950, the newer '1944 Pattern' equipment was being issued. Although it had been specifically designed for jungle use during the war, it did not see service until its very end and even then in very small quantities. Made of a lighter weave of webbing, it soon became modified by the men to make it easier and more practicable to use. Pouches were often taken off the belt and hung lower, being secured with string through the eyelets on the lower half of the belt. Its braces were seldom worn.

On day patrols, often one pouch would contain a 'Tommy cooker' and tea, and the other a bandolier or grenades. For those who carried the Bren gun, special homemade pouches to carry its magazines were worn instead. Private Bernie Elmer, a member of 5 Platoon, 'B' Company, recalled how these pouches were made:

> The tents at Wardieburn had windows in them, covered by a fine gauze. Over these was a canvas flap of the same material as the tent. These we cut off and folded over to hold two magazines for the Bren. These were great until the CSM walked in one day and asked how we'd all got these fantastic pouches, then someone coughed that we made them out of the tent. Then there was hell to pay for damaging government property![4]

Other pieces of essential kit also had to be carried. The machete was a vital piece of jungle equipment. Issued to each man, they were indispensable for hacking through vast swathes of virgin jungle in search of bandits. Some men took to adding a bead of lead along one edge to give it a bit more weight when swung.

If one was lucky, then a locally-made 'parang' was much better. These home-made knives were carried by the local trackers and were of thicker steel, usually an old recycled car spring, and featured a bone or wooden handle that often had a long length of hair tied through it. This was human hair taken, it was said, from the scalps of their opponents.

Packs were slung loose over the shoulders, ready to be ditched quickly when engaged with the enemy. In addition to shaving kit, tinned rations, mess-tin halves and cooker, rolled underneath the pack was the poncho. This was a large rubberized panel with an opening in the centre for the wearer's head. Popper studs down the sides allowed it to be gathered together into a decent rain cape, or several could be joined together to make a larger shelter. Eyelets in the corners also allowed them to be strung to trees under which men could sleep.

A small loop on the flap of the pack was designed to carry a shovel or pick, but more often than not a pair of brown canvas plimsolls was strung here to change into after patrol. Locally-made hockey boots or 'bumpers' were much favoured by the men and could be bought through the regimental contractor, Mr Hamid, in his shop inside the camp. Sometimes, though, these could be found less expensively as Private Colin Smith, a member of the mortar platoon recalled:

> All we found were three abandoned bandit packs – old British large packs covered in red stars. Inside there were the usual tins of green and red Gibbs 'Dentifrice' toothpaste, copies of Chinese magazines and several pairs of 'bumpers' – you know those old black and white canvas boots with ribbed soles. Unfortunately they were all quite small sizes but me being a size seven, I got a couple of pairs![5]

Of all jungle creatures, it was the bloodsucking leech that was the most dreaded. Men learned to look out for each other and usually a chum was on hand to cut the suckers off one's skin with a razor blade or with the lighted end of a cigarette, as Second Lieutenant Pat Bird recalled:

> It was absolutely routine to pick half a dozen off when you returned to camp in the evening. You just got used to it. Occasionally one bite would go septic, but that and what was called 'jungle sores' were a real hazard that grew worse the longer you were out there and your blood thinned. Ringworm and prickly heat were rife amongst the ORs [Other Ranks] who didn't wash well enough. Anything to do with sweating – we had it![6]

Private Ernie Guest of 8 Platoon, 'C' Company also recalled the dreaded leeches on one memorable swamp patrol near Kuala Kubu Bharu:

> We wore jungle boots that were supposed to be leech-proof but you'd be walking along and suddenly someone would shout, 'Guesty – your boots!' You would look at your boots and they would be red. The leech had got into your boot, sucked your blood and then you had squashed it and blood was oozing out. They would also get attached to your back. One of the routine things we would do is stop every hour for a smoke and a rest. We used to light up a cigarette and touch the leech with the lighted end and they'd fall off. If you tried to pull them off their teeth would still be attached and it could leave a pretty nasty sore afterwards.[7]

Trousers would not be tucked into boots but worn over the top and tied over with the long laces of the jungle boots so that they could be rolled up quickly to get at the dreaded creatures. At night men took to wearing their blue PT shorts over their jungle green trousers along with the standard issue woollen pullover as well; anything thick enough to prevent the dreaded mosquito pushing its nose through.

It was at night that the mosquito was most active. These being deadly carriers of disease, men were issued with special sprays and pastes to keep them at bay in the darkness. Special net coverings were to be worn on hands and faces, but often these were too cumbersome to put on. Men either wore their green face veil or a towel over their faces instead. It was best to sleep face-down and tuck one's hands in to keep any exposed skin to a minimum. Half a blanket helped to keep one warm when the sun disappeared and it could be rolled up in the cape when carried.

When patrols did last for more than a day, they would usually stop an hour before it got dark to give them time to make a shelter for the night. These 'bashas' would be simple affairs, with sloping roofs over which the poncho cape could be slung. The sleeping area would be cleared of all vegetation and further capes would be laid down. The rotting vegetation of the jungle floor could be surprisingly comfortable.

While a pair of men worked on the shelter, another pair would get on with supper, throwing the patrol's tins of food into a large pot. An open fire was usually made for speed, saving the precious fuel tablets for their smaller 'Tommy cookers' for boiling water for tea in the morning.

Food in the jungle was pretty much like what their forefathers had eaten during the war. The ration packs of old were shared out before the patrol set off and the contents distributed. Normally lunch was a quick affair, it being important to keep on the move. This was made simpler with the use of self-heating tins. These had a button in the lid that when pressed triggered a reaction inside that heated the contents, as Second Lieutenant Robin Farmer recalled:

> Typically, we would march about two hours, then stop for a drink of 'jungle juice'. This was a concoction the Army had provided for us which I assume had vitamins in it since it had a sort of lemony flavour. The next stop would be lunch and we had self-heating tins of stewed steak or soup, which would not create smoke, thus exposing our position. We also carried a large tin into which, in the evening, we would dump the contents of all our tins and make 'jungle stew'.[8]

The ubiquitous 'jungle stew' was also remembered by Private Tony Rogers:

> Taking the collected cans of compo rations from each man, if you are lucky you will find marks on the cans that indicate their contents. Assuming this to be so, the first can into the pot should always be the mixed vegetables, quickly followed by the boiled potatoes, stewed steak and bacon. Followed then with

steak and kidney pudding, and after stirring for a few minutes, on an open fire, gently add the pineapple chunks, fruit salad and the treacle pudding. As someone once said 'It's the bulk that matters!'[9]

Occasionally, however, food might be a little 'hit and miss', as Private Dick May of 1 Platoon, 'A' Company recalled:

> We'd been dished out tins from the boxes before going in and come supper time, everyone put forward a tin for dinner. Stew, biscuits and all that. My tin of stew seemed a bit light and with Ron's tin opener that he always had tucked in his hat, we opened it up to find it half-empty. Someone in the canning plant back home had emptied half its contents and resealed it! We couldn't blame them though. Winters at home were bad and everyone was still being rationed.[10]

At the same time as constructing a basha and getting dinner on, sentries were posted. Once the perimeters had been established, a simple system of tripwires would be placed, as Private Hugh Doran of 4 Platoon, 'B' Company recalled:

> We'd put a Mills bomb in a 50-cigarette grey 'Players' tin. Pin removed and upside down so that the lever held it there. Then string across a trip wire and hold it on a tree opposite. Any tug of the wire would pull the bomb out and let it off. We only ever had it happen a couple of times but in the morning someone always had the tricky task of replacing the pin![11]

Tea was the lifeblood of the British soldier and in Malaya this was no exception. Here army-issued tea and milk was ready-made in both powdered form or in a freeze-dried block and after getting a cup of water boiled over a 'Tommy cooker' the contents were stirred in. It was pretty bland stuff, but much appreciated. Private Tony Rogers recalled the importance of getting clean water:

> When making tea in the jungle you always had to find clear clean water. In one case a friend of mine was making tea when a man who had just come in from stag dipped his mug into the tea urn and immediately spat it out, exclaiming 'That's disgusting.' He was informed that the tea had not yet been made, but that was the colour of the water![12]

At night, the pitch-black jungle would come alive with the din of humming insects. The hours of darkness would be divided into periods of watch, usually for an hour at a time. Standing deadly still with a rifle cocked, watching for any sign of movement, soon the sentry's eyes became accustomed to the dark, but for young conscript soldiers their first solitary watch could be frightening.

Private Dick May remembered his first terrifying early-morning 'stag' duty in the jungle. His officer, the Honourable Thomas Ponsonby, was, like him, a young National

Serviceman whose descendants had served in the regiment since the 1850s. As Dick kept watch, he slept beside him. Dick remembered his stutter:

> Suddenly I heard a rustling. It was getting closer and closer until it seemed like it was just inches in front of me. This is it, I thought, and with one complete squeeze, I let rip on the Bren gun. One magazine gone in an instant and the enemy well and truly alerted. My officer emerged from under the basha: 'Wh… wh… what's up May?' 'Bandits, sir!' I replied. 'Well ok, we… we… we'll wait 'til first light and take a look. How many were there?' 'I don't know sir,' I said, 'but I heard rustling really close.'[13]

At first light, the patrol ventured forward to see what they had killed. Expecting a haul of dead bandits, they were disappointed. In front of them, some yards into the jungle, was the bullet-riddled body of a wild boar. 'Cc… cc… carry on,' said 'Hon Tom Pon'[14] and Dick and his chums started to dig a hole to bury the unfortunate animal. Second Lieutenant Robin Farmer also remembered the much-hated midnight guard duty:

> The lads hated this duty, as they found the jungle at night very intimidating, and all sorts of weird noises and shapes very menacing. The way every single one of them managed to perform the duties, despite the fact that they were obviously very scared, said a lot for their guts.[15]

Sometimes, however, the bandits would pass incredibly close, as Robin continued:

> We found some very effective concealment in some shrubs which gave us a good view of the track. We were exposed at our rear, so I told Private Jolly to face behind to protect us and said his job was 'to make sure we were not attacked from behind'. Nothing happened during the night, and once again at first light, we left the position, making sure we were gone long before the rubber-tappers came in at 6.00am in order for us to be able to return to the same spot, since it was in the middle of a busy rubber estate. As we walked back to the road, Jolly said to me, 'I didn't know they had girls as terrorists, Sir.' I replied, 'Oh yes, some of them are more vicious than the men.' 'Pretty good-looking though,' replied Jolly. 'Why? What do you mean?' 'Well two of them went past last night Sir.' 'Well why on earth didn't you fire at them?' 'Well sir, you told me to guard our rear, and as they just walked straight past and weren't doing us any harm, I left them alone!'[16]

In the morning the patrol would be on its way again. The bashas were broken up and scattered. It never took the jungle more than a few weeks to completely obliterate any trace of them ever having stopped there.

When patrols were longer, replenishment and re-supply came in by air. One notable long-range patrol by 'D' Company in the area north of Broga in 1950 required resupply by air. Dakotas dropped food and ammunition along with a crate of Tiger beer and a box of Tuborg lager. Amazingly, the bottles were unbroken.

Weaponry had also evolved. Early on, the old Mk 5 Sten proved to be ineffective for jungle warfare. It soon became clear that its 9mm ammunition lacked punch, as Corporal Don Randall of 'A' Company recalled:

> You could actually see the bullets ricocheting off their [the bandits'] webbing packs and only a .303 from a jungle carbine or the Bren would bring them down. Later we got American carbines and they were a lot better and with much more stopping power.[17]

The US-manufactured M1 and M2 carbines were much favoured by the local planters and soon their popularity spread into the army where they were issued in small numbers, normally to the patrol commander or sergeant. A reporter for *The Times* newspaper noted their popularity within the patrol, and also the difficulties of their procurement:

> A soldier's love is lavished on the American carbine. It is light, well-balanced, and ideal for jungle warfare, but there are few available because of the dollar shortage. It seems strange that there are enough dollars here to buy American cars, cosmetics and brightly-coloured neckties, but insufficient ones to buy good weapons.[18]

For all-round effectiveness and reliability, the most successful (and highly-prized) weapon was the Australian-made 9mm Owen submachine gun. Though of the same calibre as the Sten, its gravity-fed magazine was located on top of the barrel as opposed to the side, which greatly reduced stoppages. Procured in small numbers, they were very hard to come by and it was considered an honour to carry one within the patrol, as Private Bernie Elmer recalled:

> It was great, much better than that old Sten. Normally the leading scout would go first with the Owen, then behind him, the Bren-gunner with his number 2 behind. Then the rest of us – with No. 5s and someone with the EY and the sergeant or the platoon commander at the back with their carbines.[19]

The placement of specific weaponry within the patrol was crucial to its effectiveness, as Bernie continued:

> If we saw a bandit, the scout would break right and the Bren-gunner would spray the area with the Bren. The others would go left and right and the man with the EY would crouch down and fire a grenade over all of us in front.[20]

The 'EY' [Extra Yoke or Emergency] was a standard Mk III SMLE rifle, usually of Great War vintage that had a cup discharger fitted to the end of its barrel to allow it to fire a grenade. The ballistite (smokeless propellant) cartridge required to propel the grenade on its way had ferocious velocity and because of this, the woodwork along the barrel was reinforced with copper telegraph wire, soldered into place to withstand the strain. Its kick demanded that it be fired from a kneeling position, rifle butt on the floor like a mortar, though the more daring man could, if strong enough, fire it from the shoulder, though this was definitely not recommended.

A primed grenade was always carried ready in the cup, protected by a small cover to stop it falling out. The cover was for a 3in mortar and often if bandits were sighted, the grenade would be fired through the bag. For his personal weapon, the EY rifleman also carried a pistol. Private John Blench was Second Lieutenant Pat Bird's 'EY man' in 6 Platoon, 'B' Company. Pat recalled his confident handling of the weapon:

> It had a tremendous kick, and in the heat of the moment John would aim it directly at the target with devastating effect. The other problem in the jungle, of course, was that there were a lot of trees about and if the grenade were to hit a tree and bounce back, it would have the reverse effect of that desired! You needed a reliable man on the EY, and John was certainly that.[21]

The redoubtable Bren gun was the mainstay of any patrol, being able to spray the undergrowth with fire. It took a strong man to carry it and soon stretcher straps and lashings from air-drops were used to make slings to disperse its weight on longer patrols. Other members of the patrol also carried additional magazines for the weapon should they be needed.

Placed at the rear of the patrol was the signaller carrying a heavy No. 68 wireless set. His job was arguably the most important as Private Maurice Etienne, the signaller in 1 Platoon, 'A' Company recalled: 'Being a Signaller kept me out of the action most of the time. I was pushed at the back of the patrol and mostly left at base in the jungle as it was important to keep the signaller alive to keep in contact with HQ.'[22]

Second Lieutenant Robin Farmer also recalled the composition of his patrol from 12 Platoon:

> We would be led by the leading scout, normally Private Stone from Lincolnshire, a strong lad, stocky and full of guts. He was totally reliable and with common sense. Alongside him would be one of the trackers, either Chico or Banyan. Chico was young and energetic, but Banyan was a lot older and shrewd but altogether a better tracker. They were both exceedingly bloodthirsty, and their natural inclination was to headhunt! I followed, and then came three or four riflemen, Private Lumsden from Northampton, a highly intelligent grammar

school boy, who had the unenviable task of carrying the antique radio with which we were provided. Our call sign was suffixed with '4 Charlie' which denoted 12 Platoon in D Company. The set was very unreliable and it took ages to get through. Two Irish brothers were both corporals in the platoon, tall, good-looking and strong lads called Kelly. I was always glad to have them with me. They were both carrying Owen guns, the Australian version of the Sten gun, and much more robust and reliable. The riflemen included Potter, Newsome, Rush, Welham, Minter and Large.[23]

When the patrol was over, the signaller would send word that they required collection. Usually a truck would be dispatched as soon as possible to meet the patrol at the location given. No drivers ever went out alone and if the area was known to be the least bit hostile, a scout car would also be sent.

The battalion possessed a number of Humber and Daimler Dingo scout cars. Armed with either twin Vickers 'K' guns or double Bren guns with larger 100-round drum magazines, their fire could be called upon to 'rake' areas of the jungle if required.

The battalion also inherited a set of decaying vehicles for use in a number of roles. The most popular and versatile were the US-built Dodge WC52 'weapon carriers' that could carry a complete patrol's worth of men out on operations. By far the most unpopular vehicle was an armoured truck known as 'the Pig' or the 'Ark Royal'. Men hated travelling in its confined sweltering interior, and with its entry and exit being from double doors at the rear, men were naturally worried should a convoy be ambushed and they could not escape. Later it would be used for the ferrying of rations and supplies from a depot near Kuala Lumpur to the battalion's outstations.

Following a tradition that was started in North-West Europe during the war, the battalion's vehicles were named after regimental battle honours and could be seen sporting such names as 'Gibraltar', 'Minden', 'Le Cateau', 'Suvla', 'Somme' and 'Arras'.

'The Pig' was originally named 'Birkenhead'; not a regimental battle honour, but in remembrance of when troops of the regiment stood fast on the deck of the sinking troopship *Birkenhead*, allowing women and children to be rescued first. Later, when someone mentioned that this was not the most appropriate name for such a disliked vehicle, it was renamed 'Neuve Chapelle'.

When the patrol returned to camp, there was always the weapons check. Men were lined up and breaches were opened and barrels examined. Those who had been carrying grenades had to lay them at their feet before the patrol commander checked that all was in order and that all the pins were present.

The patrol would march to the armoury where their arms and ammunition were handed in. The armoury storeman Private Ross, who was an accomplished artist, would check off the weapons and confirm the serial numbers. Only when all were accounted for was the platoon commander informed and the men dismissed, and then the NAAFI was 'on limits' to them.

However, despite these rigorous weapon checks, unfortunate incidents did occur. One entirely accidental mistake cost a newly-arrived subaltern, Second Lieutenant Tony Cobbold, a severe reprimand from the CO, as Private Dick May recalled:

> He was getting out of the scout car when the lanyard that fired the double Brens on top got caught around his holster. These were so you could fire the guns from inside the car. Anyway, accidentally, as he jumped down, he pulled the cord and raked the entire square in front of Battalion HQ with machine-gun fire, nearly killing Ian Wight in the process who was walking across to his office and dived head-first into the flower bed![24]

Tony served the longest time of any officer of the regiment in Malaya. He later became honorary curator of the regimental museum and was a staunch supporter of the Old Comrades Association.

After a long and wearisome patrol a drink was looked forward to. Tiger Beer was the favoured brew of many a soldier in Malaya. Quite often their catchy slogan was penned at the end of letters home, as it was always 'Time for a Tiger'. 'ABC Anchor' was another popular brand of lager, its initials stood for the 'Archipelago Brewing Company'.

(**Right**) Upon arrival in Malaya the training continued at a pace. It was here that the men were introduced to the weapons with which they were to fight. Though all knew the Bren gun and Sten gun from their basic training at home, most were unfamiliar with the shorter No. 5 rifle known as the 'jungle carbine'. Private Last of 3 Platoon, 'A' Company, selected to be an EY rifleman, hones his shooting skills with a .38 service revolver. A pistol was carried as the personal weapon of the 'EY' man.

(**Opposite, above**) A group shot of 3 Platoon on a jungle range. The variety of weapons that the 'average' patrol would carry can be seen here: five Owens, three Brens, one EY rifle and four No. 5 rifles. The two Iban trackers are armed with No. 4 rifles.

(**Opposite, below**) An early 'C' Company patrol at Broga. This photograph was taken during Operation LOWESTOFT in September 1949. Here the men are drawn up in platoon groups to be briefed about the operation. The building in the background was the village school. These men wear white bandages in their jungle hats for identification.

✂ DISCOVER MORE ABOUT PEN & SWORD BOOKS

Pen & Sword Books have over 4000 books currently available, our imprints include; Aviation, Naval, Military, Archaeology, Transport, Frontline, Seaforth and the Battleground series, and we cover all periods of history on land, sea and air.

Can we stay in touch? From time to time we'd like to send you our latest catalogues, promotions and special offers by post. If you would prefer not to receive these, please tick this box. ☐

We also think you'd enjoy some of the latest products and offers by post from our trusted partners: companies operating in the clothing, collectables, food & wine, gardening, gadgets & entertainment, health & beauty, household goods, and home interiors categories. If you would like to receive these by post, please tick this box. ☐

We respect your privacy. We use personal information you provide us with to send you information about our products, maintain records and for marketing purposes. For more information explaining how we use your information please see our privacy policy at www.pen-and-sword.co.uk/privacy. You can opt out of our mailing list at any time via our website or by calling 01226 734222.

Mr/Mrs/Ms ....

Address...

Postcode................ Email address........................

Website: www.pen-and-sword.co.uk Email: enquiries@pen-and-sword.co.uk
Telephone: 01226 734555   Fax: 01226 734438
Stay in touch: facebook.com/penandswordbooks or follow us on Twitter @penswordbooks

Freepost Plus RTKE-RGRJ-KTTX
Pen & Sword Books Ltd
47 Church Street
BARNSLEY
S70 2AS

(**Opposite, above**) Elements of 'D' Company move out from the battalion base at Kajang on a large-scale patrol into the jungle. The fourth vehicle in line was the much-hated armoured truck known as 'the Pig'. A Humber scout car brings up the rear of the convoy armed with twin Vickers 'K' guns.

(**Above**) Swiftness was the key to success on operations. Sometimes when the call came the men of the Standby Platoon had to be dumped at their entry point in the jungle as quickly as possible to pick up the chase. Here a platoon of 'A' Company are forced to alight from their transport while it is still moving, for just minutes before information had been received that the bandits were sabotaging the rubber trees on the Rasa Estate.

(**Opposite, below**) An early patrol of 10 Platoon, 'D' Company on a logging plantation at Semenyih. In the early days of their tour the battalion kept to the tracks, but it was soon realized that it would be necessary to take the fight to the terrorists, deep in their jungle camps.

(**Opposite, above**) A short day patrol of 'A' Company comes back into camp in September 1949. At first these patrols were usually sent out close to the perimeter of Wardieburn Camp, whose huts can be seen in the background. They helped to acclimatize the men to the rigours of the longer patrolling that lay ahead.

(**Opposite, below**) The long grass or 'lalang' grew thick and fast on the jungle's edge in the swampy areas. Usually this was the toughest part of the initial journey when, with no cover from the sun, the leading scout wielded his machete to hack his way through. This grass was so thick that it was easy to get lost if you didn't follow the man in front; here just his hat is visible above the grass in the centre.

(**Above**) The first 'real' jungle to be reached once the grass was conquered was usually 'secondary' jungle: jungle that had at some time been cultivated but had been partly allowed to revert to nature. Here 3 Platoon moves unhindered onto the edge of a young rubber plantation. The tree in the foreground has recently been tapped and is 'weeping'.

(**Opposite, above**) It was on the plantations that the first tappers were seen. Predominantly Chinese, they carried pails over their shoulders in which they would collect natural latex tapped from the rubber trees. Constant checks had to be made on these tappers, many of whom sympathized with the terrorists' cause and carried messages and supplies for them, usually hidden in their buckets.

(**Opposite, below**) Making good use of a jungle track, the patrol could cover much more ground, but here they were more susceptible to a bandit attack, hence the distance between men. If bandits were seen, fire discipline was essential lest an over-enthusiastic soldier should accidentally fire on his comrades.

(**Above**) An Indian rubber tapper on the Tarun Estate has his pockets checked by a member of 'A' Company. In his hand he carries a distinctive curved knife to scribe the rubber trees to release the natural latex. Along with the Chinese, large numbers of Indians and local Tamils also worked on the plantations.

A brief stop to make a quick cup of tea. Here a Fijian guide on a 'D' Company patrol gets a mess tin of water up to the boil while the rest of the patrol holds back on the track. A stop was usually made for ten minutes in every hour for a drink and a chance for the men to smoke. Soon, with the fire extinguished, they would be off again.

Another patrol, another stop. Here Major Jack Devey commanding 'C' Company pauses to cover his hands in mosquito repellent; the double-ended tube containing it can be seen in his left hand. Devey was a regular officer of the Northamptonshire Regiment who joined 1st Suffolk in Greece in 1949. He was later wounded in the arm by bandit fire when on patrol in January 1950.

'Fearless' officer wins jungle MC

Second Lieutenant John Starling, Suffolk Regt., has been awarded the M.C. for gallantry in leading two jungle attacks near Kuala Lumpur, Malaya.

His mother, Mrs. Mildred Starling, of French's-road, Cambridge, said yesterday that she was not surprised by the news.

"My son is absolutely fearless," she said. "He is as keen as mustard on his Army career."

Captain 'Joe' Starling photographed at the regimental depot in 1953. For his actions on a patrol north of Kuala Lumpur in November 1949 he was awarded the Military Cross; the first to be won by an officer of the battalion in Malaya. By the end of their tour a further eight had been won, along with two DSOs, one DCM, three MMs and three BEMs.

The first mention of 'Joe' Starling's award did not attract much attention in the UK newspapers. Later as their success in Malaya increased, the Battalion shared equal press coverage both at home and abroad with details of their exploits.

Several members of the patrol that won 'Joe' his MC were young bandsmen who had only been sent out due to a shortage of available men. Bandsman Michael Swann, who later died of wounds received that day, was a contemporary of Bandsman Dave Arthur (left). Dave and 'Mickey' were two of five 'boys' who enlisted into the Regiment in 1945 and all had consecutive regimental service numbers. Dave's bandsman's badge can just be seen here on the sleeve of his aertex jungle shirt. Dave was later a member of the 'Suffolk Concert Band' formed in 1967 from a nucleus of ex-Suffolk Regiment musicians.

(**Above, left**) Thirsty work. Here 'Sonny' Jim or 'Tiger' Horton of 1 Platoon, 'A' Company drinks from his aluminium water bottle. Jim was often the leading scout for his patrol, armed with an Owen gun. The weapon had straight magazines like its British equivalent the Sten that were carried in a three-compartment pouch as seen here. He has removed the rubber pads on the inside of his jungle boots that often chafed on long patrols.

(**Above, right**) A pause for a quick bite to eat, although this member of 10 Platoon doesn't seem too impressed with the issue biscuits he's been given from the fourteen-man ration crate. These 'biscuits' were a tough form of cracker that were designed to be a substitute for bread when eaten with the other tinned foodstuffs that the crate contained. There were different menu options within each crate.

(**Opposite, above**) A pause on a rubber estate to allow the native tracker to get coconuts for the patrol. Some soldiers had a taste for them and others disliked them, but here a soldier can be seen kneeling and using his machete in an attempt to hack one open to get at its milk.

(**Opposite, below**) A Bren-gunner of 4 Platoon, 'B' Company sits quietly having a smoke during a pause on a day patrol in 1950. 'One-day ops' were designed to be of four to six hours' duration and did not require the men to carry rations or packs for an overnight stay in the jungle.

An early (and well-stocked) 'D' Company patrol in 1949 operating north of the Batu Caves. This appears to be the evening meal in preparation. The tins from the ration crate have been pooled and an old biscuit tin is heating gently over an open fire, no doubt containing the ubiquitous 'jungle stew'. In the foreground, two members of the patrol appear to be unwrapping packets of biscuits.

Off again as soon as possible, this 4 Platoon patrol now breaks into fairly hilly country near Ampang. As the patrol moves into uncultivated jungle, the ferns have already enveloped the leading scout just yards in front. In the middle, Private Brian Allen checks his Bren before following the scout into the 'ulu' (deserted territory).

A well-used map of the Batu Arang area as carried by Second Lieutenant Robin Farmer with four areas marked that he was to patrol. He kept it folded in a flat cigarette tin. In reality, these 1:25000 scale maps were pretty useless for patrols, except to gain heights and gradients if they were known.

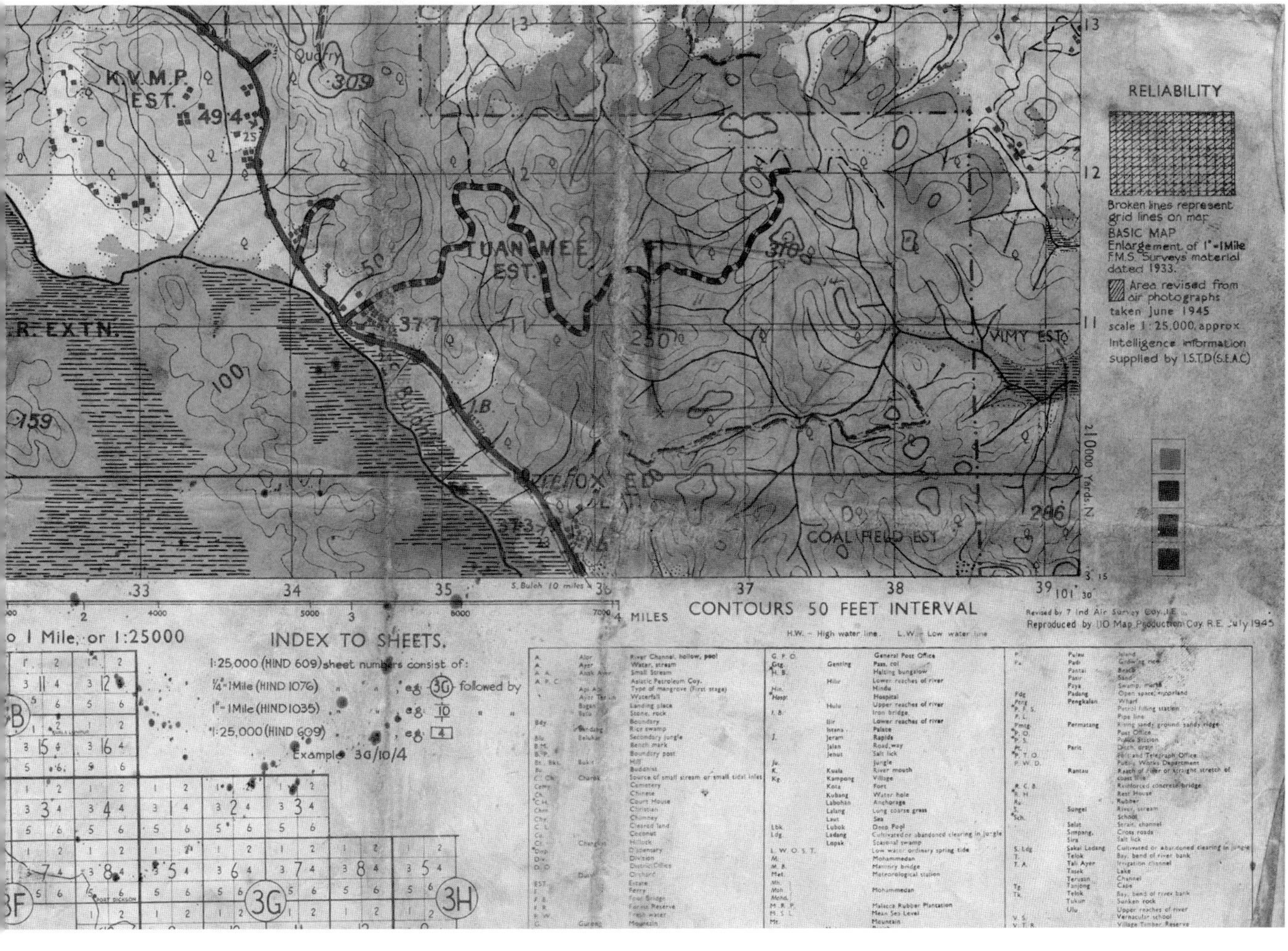

(**Opposite, above**) A welcome break from jungle patrolling was a search of the tin mines and isolated rubber factories. Here a member of 1 Platoon, 'A' Company photographed the feat of bamboo engineering that was a tin mine at Broga. The man-made structure here took the washed spoil away from the mine after the natural tin had been extracted.

(**Opposite, below**) A tough patrol in the swamps around Dengkil, south of Kuala Lumpur in early 1951. Here men pause for a photograph to be taken by Private Sid Brace of 6 Platoon, 'B' Company. Ankle-deep in swampy, mosquito-infested water and clearly exhausted, his comrades find it hard to raise a smile.

(**Above**) Deep under the jungle canopy, almost completely shaded from the sun, Private John Hopkins of 10 Platoon, 'D' Company poses with a fellow patrol member. On this particular patrol John carries the redoubtable Bren gun, a weapon that could become heavy on longer patrols, but here John uses a webbing stretcher strap to help him spread its weight more comfortably.

(**Opposite, above left**) Breaking into a squatter settlement in a jungle clearing, a patrol of 3 Platoon performs a routine search of the huts for arms and ammunition. Quite often the native Malay aborigines lived in tree houses that were nicknamed 'Kajang council houses'. Here Corporal Cox examines a Chinese lady's washing for any contraband. She seems amused at his trying to decipher her identity papers.

(**Opposite, above right**) A member of 'B' Company checks the papers of a young Chinese girl as she taps the rubber from a nearby tree.

(**Opposite, below**) After trudging onwards, another stop and a chance for a smoke and a drink. In mountainous country near Klang, men of 'B' Company pause for a few minutes. The exhaustion of a long and uneventful patrol is evident on their faces, although the man in the foreground is still just smiling.

(**Above**) The ever-cheerful Private Jackson. A rifleman in 5 Platoon, 'B' Company, he pauses while on a patrol through a logging trail in the Kuala Langat South Swamp. Jackson is armed with the 'jungle carbine', a shorter variant of the No. 4 rifle. It had a flash eliminator on the end of its barrel and a stout rubber pad on the end of its butt to compensate its firer for the large increase in recoil.

On the same patrol Private Foyster, the EY rifleman, rests for a few minutes. A craze went around 5 Platoon in late 1950 of putting one's girlfriend's name on the brim of a jungle hat. This, however, ceased when one man received a 'Dear John' letter from home, but apparently Private Foyster did later marry Doreen, who was a nurse in Great Yarmouth. He carries a .38 pistol should they come under attack and his stock of grenades is exhausted. A grenade was always carried primed and ready in the cup discharger, covered here with a tied rubberized bag.

Another member of that patrol, Private Cooper, makes contact with base during a routine wireless check. The old wartime No. 18 wireless set (later improved and renumbered as No. 68) was notoriously unreliable in the jungle. Just as in North-West Europe, any form of moisture played havoc with its delicate valves. Its range was also limited and on longer patrols contact was frequently lost. Most patrols carried Very pistols and coloured flares to summon urgent assistance if the set failed to operate. In the background, a bare-chested Corporal Atkins smiles for the camera.

The making of a 'basha' or shelter just before darkness set in. Here men of 'B' Company have cleared away a patch of scrub and have slung their waterproof ponchos up to make a shelter. With equipment ditched and stowed inside, Private 'Sperry' Free smiles for the camera, while a colleague (just out of shot) holds a cup of recently-brewed tea in his aluminium mug. A towel or 'sweat rag' is drying on one branch in the foreground, while a blackened mess tin is hung from another.

(**Opposite, above**) Jungle dinner. Privates Ron Newlands and John Blench of 6 Platoon, 'B' Company are captured here having their evening meal. Ron waits ready with his mess tin half for his tin of self-heating Heinz oxtail soup to come up to temperature. A button in the can was depressed, triggering a reaction inside to heat the contents. Usually within two minutes it was hot enough to eat. John slackens his thirst with a drink from a coconut.

(**Opposite, below**) Members of 5 Platoon in their jungle camp stop for their evening meal. On the right, Private Richard Baldwin keeps an eye on the three mess tins of supper cooking over an open fire. Each man carried his two halves of the mess tin in the large pockets on either side of his pack.

(**Above**) Frantic activity by members of 5 Platoon to build their bashas before the onset of darkness. Most men carried ropes for fording fast-flowing jungle streams, but here they are strung between trees over which their poncho capes could be draped. Despite the humidity, at least two of the men seen here wear the issue woollen pullovers. In the foreground, the photographer's jungle hat is perched on a twig.

(**Above**) Happy with his accommodation for the night, this member of 5 Platoon relaxes with a cigarette. He has already removed his jungle boots and has changed into a dry and more comfortable pair of canvas PT shoes. In the foreground are his colleague's small pack, machete (in its sheath) and a length of coiled rope.

(**Opposite, above**) As the patrol now gets their heads down to sleep, the sentries are alone. Here an Owen-gunner of 'B' Company lies crouched in the undergrowth. Were it not for the shield on his jungle hat bearing the letter 'B' and the magazine of his weapon, he has virtually merged into the jungle's shadows. Night-time 'stag' could be a daunting and frightening time for young soldiers, for in the darkness the jungle came alive with the din of hundreds of howling and buzzing creatures.

(**Opposite, below**) Men of 4 Platoon, 'B' Company are paraded for the cameras to illustrate the various weapons that the Battalion carried in action. Private Hugh Doran, second left, carries an M2 Carbine, though he later recalled, he never carried one and that 'it was thrust at me for the benefit of the camera!'

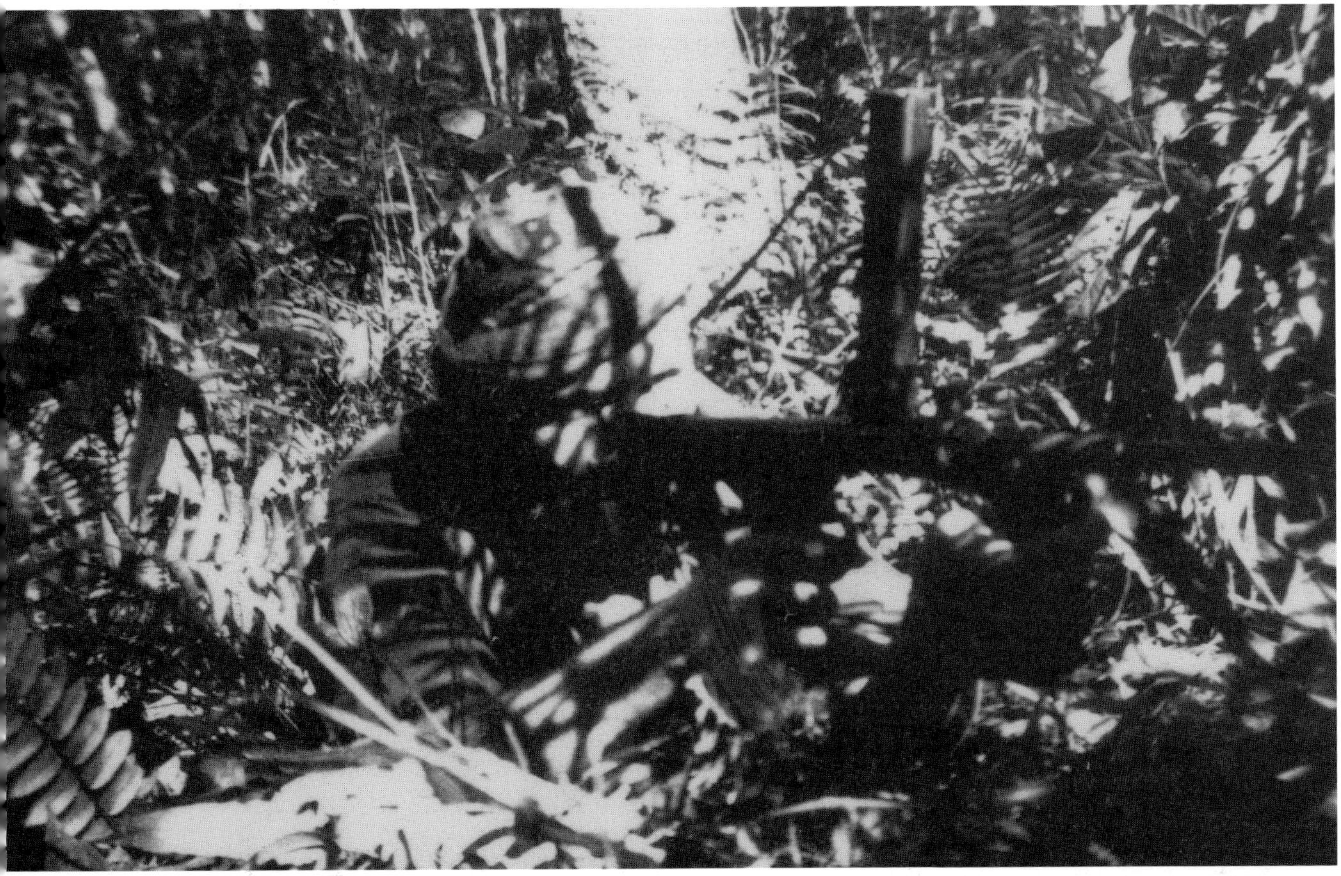

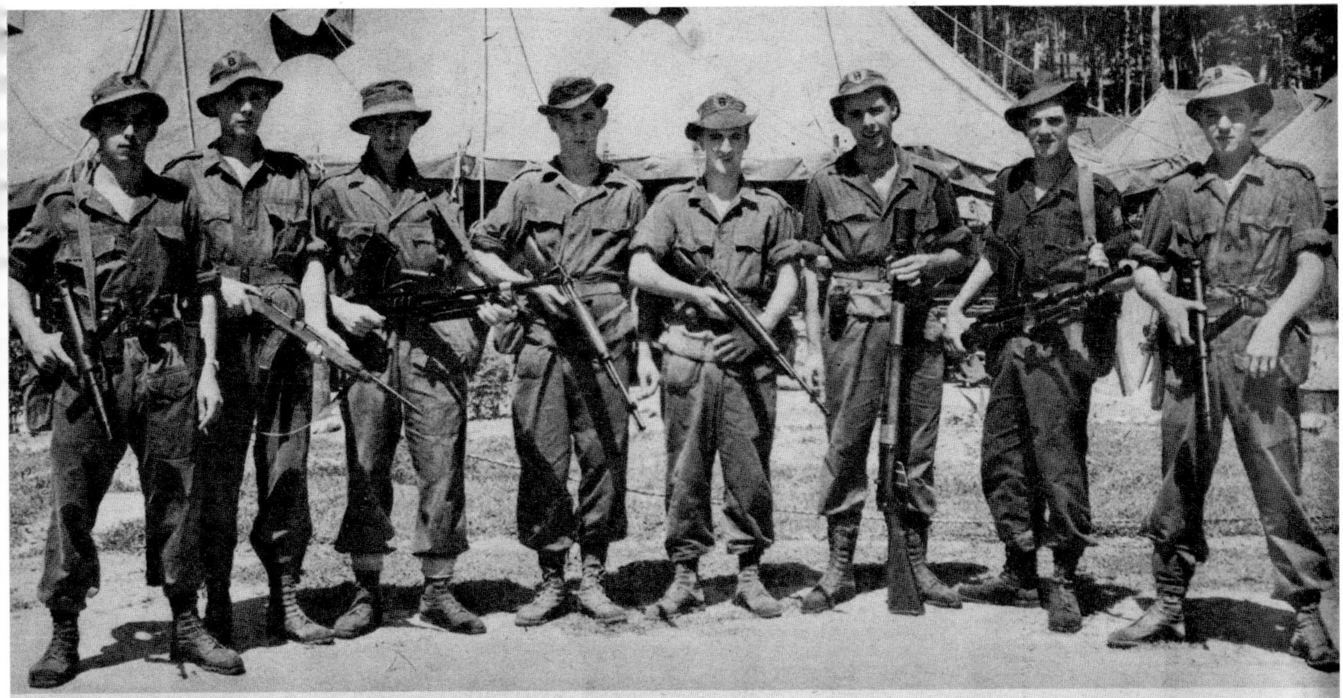

How the Suffolks go armed on jungle patrol. From left to right, in order of march: Owen gun, American carbine, Bren, two No. 5 rifles, No. 1 rifle with cup discharger, Bren and Owen gun.

WAR OF MANY WEAPONS

IN Malaya today there is probably a greater variety of small arms in use than anywhere else in the world.

The security forces — Army and Police — alone have an

(**Above, left**) Before moving off again the following morning, a chance to check weaponry and equipment. Here a member of 12 Platoon, 'D' Company sharpens his machete with a sharpening stone. The machete was as important as any weapon and the progress of the patrol relied on the sharpness of its blade and the strength of its user to hack through the undergrowth.

(**Above, right**) For the adventurous, if time permitted a local stream could offer the chance of a wash down and shave. Later such actions were discouraged when a party of bandits stalking a patrol of the Cameronians wounded three men while they were bathing.

(**Right**) Private Halls of 10 Platoon, 'D' Company waits to start off on patrol again. In front of him is the patrol's No. 18 wireless set, complete with aerials in the pouch and the signals satchel on top. The loop antenna wire can be seen wound on top. Its carrier, Private John Hopkins who took the photograph, has wrapped his poncho cape around its supporting frame to ease its heavy load. In the foreground is the rarely-seen silenced version of the Mk II Sten gun. Its silencer is wrapped in a laced canvas cover. The EY rifle with its cup discharger wrapped in a waterproof bag can also be seen along with John's camera case.

Heading back from patrol, men of 'B' Company exit a rubber plantation on their way back to camp. In front, Private 'Spud' Murphy wades through the water carrying his EY rifle.

(**Opposite, above**) After trekking for some hours, a bandit camp is discovered. More often than not these had already been abandoned, but a thorough search is still made before the site is destroyed and the patrol moves on. Rarely did men set fire to the bandit bashas lest it draw attention to their activities. Within a few weeks the jungle's undergrowth would have obliterated any traces of its existence.

(**Above**) A well-constructed bandit hut is discovered on the extreme edge of a rubber plantation. With a team effort, men of 3 Platoon destroy the structure lest it be used again as a launch-pad for another terrorist raid on the plantation. The man second left wears a home-made pouch on the rear of his belt carrying four thirty-round magazines for the Bren gun.

(**Opposite, below**) A brief pause before moving on again. A Bren-gunner of 4 Platoon, 'B' Company keeps a look. His jungle hat bears a yellow rectangle, an early form of platoon identification.

Ron Embleton, a much noted illustrator of the 1960s and 1970s, served his National Service with 1st Suffolk in Malaya. The editor of the *Suffolk Regimental Gazette* correctly prophesied in 1950 that great things lay ahead for him, for he went on to paint the end credits to the TV series *Captain Scarlet and the Mysterons* and later illustrated countless comics and books throughout his career.

The only cartoon that Ron Embleton had published in the Regimental Journal. His eye for detail is clear and his sketch illustrates clearly the older style of wartime webbing that was worn in the early months of the Battalion's tour in 1949–50.

On the fourth or fifth day of a longer patrol, men of 8 Platoon, 'C' Company wait by a jungle clearing for an air-drop from the circling DC-3 Dakota aircraft. Having arrived at the prearranged spot during the scheduled time zone, contact with the aircraft would be made by radio on the prearranged frequency. The dropping zone would be marked by smoke, or if space permitted, a coloured recognition panel was pinned out on the jungle floor.

(**Above**) Receiving a drop in the confines of the jungle could present problems. If the panniers or the canister dropped into thick jungle, it might require several hours of hacking through to reach it. Here a wicker pannier hangs in a tree, ready to be claimed, but although they are within 15ft of the parachute's canopy, it would still take another half an hour of tough machete work to reach it.

(**Opposite, above**) When contact with the enemy came, it was swift and fleeting and for many, very rarely lasted longer than a minute or so. Here, on an early patrol of 'C' Company at Broga in September 1949, Corporal 'Biff' Brown of 7 Platoon brings in a captured bandit. During these early days, the battalion still wore the wartime pattern of webbing, scrubbed to a lighter shade that contrasted with their jungle green uniform.

(**Opposite, below**) A similar early patrol at the same time resulted in four more bandits being taken prisoner by a patrol of 9 Platoon, 'C' Company. Standing in the centre guarding the prisoners is Sergeant Ashdown armed with a 9mm Mk V Sten gun. Sergeant Ashdown was later killed on patrol on 6 August 1950.

(**Opposite, above**) Another photograph taken of Corporal Brown (right) and Corporal Hambling, with the dead bodies of three bandits.

(**Opposite, below**) In the early days of patrolling, if a 'kill' was made, after a photograph was taken and the fingerprints of the dead terrorist recorded, a grave was dug in the jungle and the body buried there. Later when it became necessary to prove to the locals that a bandit had indeed been killed, all bodies were brought out for positive identification by the police. Here, in a gruesome task, three bandits are being exhumed from their jungle grave by men of 7 Platoon. This action resulted in the platoon gaining themselves the name of 'The Gravediggers'.

(**Above**) The bodies of dead bandits were usually tied to a stout branch and carried out to a pick-up point from where they would be collected and taken to the police station for identification. The typical bandit uniform of khaki drill shirt and trousers can be seen here, worn with long puttees and canvas and rubber ankle boots. His distinctive five-pointed cap would have been swiftly 'souvenired' by a member of the patrol.

At the rendezvous point and awaiting transport, the body of the bandit is left on its pole awaiting collection. When the truck arrived, the bodies would be loaded up and the patrol climbed aboard in what space remained for the journey back to camp.

Arriving back in the village, the dead and captured terrorists cause much interest among the local inhabitants. It was important to observe those who crowded around to see any emotions that might portray a bandit in civilian dress or sympathizer in the crowd. Here the captured terrorists caught by Corporal Brown's patrol are unloaded with hands tied to be escorted to the police station.

A patrol is transported back to camp in the armoured truck known as 'the Pig'. Its interior was hot and cramped and the men hated travelling in it. The wireless-operator and the Bren-gunner await assistance to climb aboard with their heavy loads. Private Tony Rogers recalled how they all hated travelling in this vehicle: 'Chugging up the Seremban Pass in first gear at around 3mph thinking we'd be ambushed at any moment!'

65

(**Above**) A patrol of 'A' Company makes their way back to camp through the centre of Kajang. The patrol commander, Major Bob 'Beever' Martin, stands at the back, while in the centre Private Broom stares into the camera. Most seem happy to have completed yet another patrol, but Private Ted Monk, sitting right, seems none too happy.

(**Opposite, above**) A frontal view of a similar truck photographed at Wardieburn Camp. The driver's cab was protected with thin armour plate, and special additional screens gave limited protection to the men travelling in the rear. All battalion vehicles carried the sign of the 18th Independent Infantry Brigade: a crossed white kukri and bayonet on a red rectangle, and a yellow regimental castle and key.

(**Opposite, below**) Awaiting transport back to camp and time for a photograph with chums. Here men of 5 Platoon pose for Private 'Bernie' Elmer's camera. A wide variety of weaponry can be seen here including a Very pistol carried in its leather shoulder holster around the waist of the rifleman on the right. All have two days' growth of beard, not having shaved for forty-eight hours.

A pause for tea and for Second Lieutenant Bob Godfrey to capture his Batman, Private Derek Hexter enjoying a cup. It was not surprising given his hometown of Dagenham in Essex, that Derek later worked for Ford Motors at their assembly plant there.

Sergeant Robert Fowler poses with his trademark pipe in a Daimler Dingo scout car named 'Gaza' after the regimental battle honour of 1917. 'Bob' Fowler was awarded the Military Medal for actions at Rawang in August 1951. His patrol of 1 Platoon, 'A' Company defeated a vastly superior bandit force without any casualties. His citation noted that 'his leadership and bearing throughout the engagement were of the highest order, and his determination to close with and inflict casualties was an example for all.'

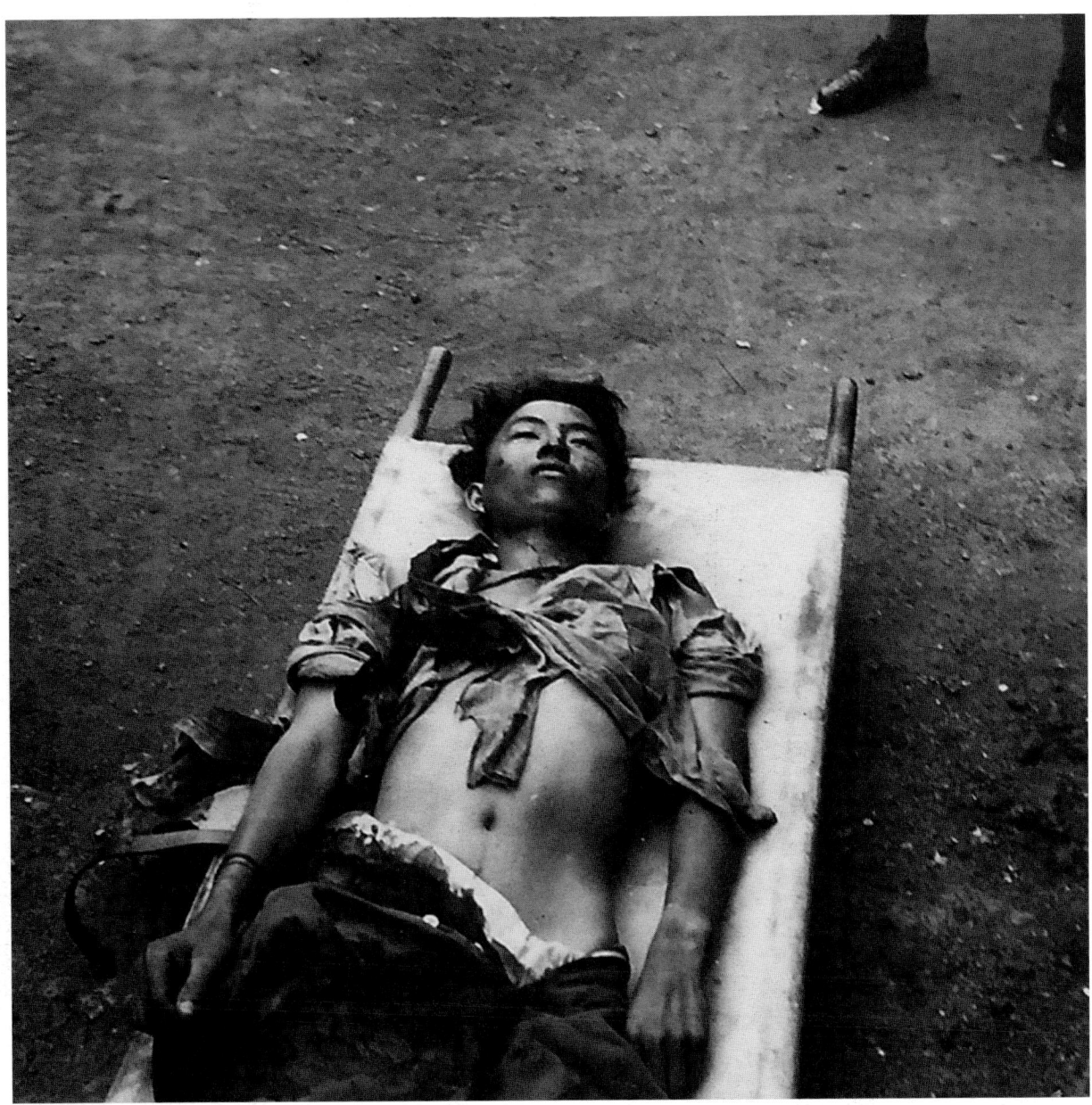
A dead bandit killed on patrol in March 1950 lays on a stretcher outside the police station at Kajang ready to be identified.

(**Above**) Off patrol in the centre of Kajang and already changed into comfy footwear, this member of 3 Platoon awaits transport back to base. This photograph offers a good view of the Australian 9mm Owen gun that he carries as his personal weapon. He also carries additional .303 ammunition for his comrades in a bandolier tied around his waist. In the background a local truck is delivering F&N Orange Crush, a popular soft drink, to a local bar. Its motto 'Famous For Flavour' can be seen painted on its bumper.

(**Opposite**) The battalion's Mortar Platoon in action at night. The 3in mortar was a useful tool in the jungle if one was keen to force bandits to move in a particular direction or one had specific reliable information about the position of a bandit camp. For the bandits deep in the jungle with no similar weapons with which to retaliate, the mortar was a psychological death blow that could fall on them at any time.

At the end of their first months of operations, the battalion was granted a few days of staggered rest and recuperation on the coast at Port Dickson. Here, leaning from the train window, Private John Hopkins of 10 Platoon, 'D' Company looks out at another train derailed by the bandits. Malaya's single-track railways made swift recovery an impossibility without closing the line for several days. Often trains were left where they had been derailed.

On the beach at Port Dickson, 10 Platoon are seen with their then platoon commander, Lieutenant 'Joe' Starling. Joe would later become the training major at the regimental depot before joining the Parachute Regiment. He retired in 1982, having reached the rank of brigadier.

Chapter Three

The Upper Hand

In early 1950 the battalion found itself being split up in various locations around Kuala Lumpur. 'A' Company returned from Kajang in the early New Year to Sungei Besi. 'B' Company was stationed at Batu Arang approximately 15 miles north of Kuala Lumpur where they guarded the coal mines from attack.

Though they were separated from the battalion for more than three months, 'B' Company's isolation did have some advantages. Being close to the Selangor Golf Club, every Wednesday they had the use of the club swimming pool and after several days of patrolling, a dip (boots and all) was greatly appreciated.

'C' Company swapped places with 'A' Company in Kajang and started a determined campaign in conjunction with the Green Howards against the bandits. Its commander Major Jack Devey, famous for his imposing 'Boer War' moustache, made contact with bandits on 13 January. In the action that followed three bandits were killed, with Major Devey being shot through the right forearm. Sergeant Thomas and Corporal Harris were also wounded.

'D' Company, now at Kajang, made few contacts with the bandits, though on 26 February a patrol of 12 Platoon at Broga killed three bandits after a short sharp fight. For their actions here Lieutenant 'Jimmy' Kelly was awarded the Military Cross and Lance Corporal Dennis Wicks the Military Medal. The patrol was one of many that were now of such duration that they necessitated being resupplied by air.

With an increase in the number of patrols being mounted by the battalion, the press was now being used more and more as a way of getting the message home to the bandits that the security forces were hard on their heels. The terrorists still relied heavily on their networks of sympathizers who lived in the villages on the jungle's edge and they soon knew from local newspapers that the Battalion meant business:

> Over six months have passed since then and the Kajang communists and the Suffolks have come to know a great deal about each other. The stage has been set, and the play has commenced on an almost personal private war between Mr. Liew and Lieut. Col. I.L. Wight commanding the Suffolks. So far Col. Wight's men have killed 12 of Liew's followers and captured three.[1]

By continually putting references to the actions of the army in the press, the bandits could see that one by one, their supply lines were being cut. This effective psychological campaign also drew unintentional side-effects. By naming the battalion for their actions, it brought attention to their presence in their various locations around Selangor.

This media campaign, however, produced a humorous counter-effect, for soon posters went up around the back streets of Kuala Lumpur offering a reward for the capture of the Suffolk Regiment. The terrorists had now placed their own bounties on the heads of many senior members of the battalion!

In the spring of 1950 the pace steadily quickened. The arrival in Malaya in April of Lieutenant General Sir Harold Briggs as Director of Operations changed the way the battalion was to operate. Briggs was keen, first and foremost, to develop and strengthen the links between the police and the armed forces.

Up to this point the police somewhat resented the arrival of the army to assist them, seeing it as an admission of their failure to overcome the terrorist networks. The army was ambivalent about the police but felt that they had often failed to act upon good information swiftly, concentrating instead on damage and attacks to European plantations and settlements.

Briggs was also determined to split the terrorists off from their supply routes. He knew that they relied heavily on the local squatters and the largely Chinese settlers who lived on the edges of the jungle. A proportion of these were already members of an underground communist movement, the 'Min Yuen', who supplied food and arms for the terrorists. Often, though, innocent peasants were coerced by a brutal regime of terror and fear to assist the terrorists who would steal what they could not take peacefully from them.

Though controversial at the time, Briggs' plan was to collect together all the squatters and settlers from the edges of the jungle and rehouse them in specially-built camps. Here they would be free from terrorist interference, giving the security forces the freedom to operate with the minimum of hindrance, deep into the jungle.

These camps or 'kampongs' had entertainment and amenities and were run by elected committees responsible to the civil powers. Under the control of armed Malay Home Guards, though the camps had wire and watchtowers, they served their purpose. Briggs knew that by depriving the bandits of many of their supplies, he would force them to retreat deeper into the jungle where he could deal with them. He knew they would not be audacious enough to bring their fight into the towns.

Overall the 'Briggs' Plan' was successful in that it convinced the local immigrant Chinese that the Federated Government cared about their welfare and that it wished to integrate them with the local population of native Malays.

In order for Briggs' plan to work, it would mean that patrolling would intensify and that the battalion would, at least for the immediate future, remain split in its various locations. In an attempt to get newly-arrived men acclimatized to the jungle more quickly, a series of 'one-day ops' was established and these proved highly successful in reducing the 'school time' that a newly-arrived soldier needed to get into the groove of active operations.

Throughout August and September 1950, the battalion was involved in no fewer than eight large-scale operations, each designed to sweep specific areas. Operations COGGESHALL, CHELMSFORD, DRINKSTONE, DECIMATE, DUNMOW, ASBAB, DOOMSDAY and CONCLUSION met with mixed results but placed considerable strain on the battalion, which now had three or four patrols out every day. To keep up with the demands of actively patrolling as large an area as possible, patrol size had to be reduced, sometimes to as few as four men. Private Maurice Etienne recalled the situation:

> We were very short of men in the Regiment and often patrols of four or five men were sent out usually for one day and no signaller was required. Most other patrols were ten to twelve men for anything up to five or six days, although I myself had been out for two weeks but as we had to carry our food it was very difficult and we got very hungry. I weighed my pack before I went out on patrol – 96lb [43.5kg] plus rifle and fifty rounds of .303 – just try walking in the jungle with that load![2]

As many men were soon to realize, patrolling was all about endurance, mental agility and above all perseverance. Constant patrolling taught men to move silently and to look out for small, often unnoticeable signs of disturbance in the undergrowth and trees. More importantly, it also taught men to look after each other, as Private Tony Coote of 3 Platoon, 'A' Company recalled:

> Survival is paramount and that was all there was to it. Kill or be killed, sad to say, but very true. If you did not watch your step, you could land in very hot water indeed, not just from your sergeant, but from the lads you were with, for one wrong move from you could endanger all their lives.[3]

In permanently damp kit with heavy packs and only a small bush hat to shield against the piercing sun, these young men, far away from home, stomped their way through their service, ever cheerful. For many 19- and 20-year-old soldiers, the jungle campaign was a private campaign and one that fostered the greatest and most enduring of friendships between comrades. Lieutenant Colonel Ian Wight noted the difficulties he had to overcome with the young men he had under his command:

> Our main problem was to accustom the young National Servicemen to live in the jungle. To a lad of eighteen from an urban background, the first time in the jungle is a frightening experience, especially at night. The blackness of the night that is alarmingly illuminated by buzzing fireflies and the phosphorescence of rotting vegetation. The stillness of the night is broken by cries of nocturnal

animals and bats; these and his own fears surround the lonely sentry. The first lesson to be learnt is that besides being frightening, the jungle can be a friend. Water is abundant, and he must learn how to move silently through trees and the lalang (overgrown cut-down trees) and his weapon must always be ready to fire. He must be supremely fit, have confidence in his leaders and comrades and, above all, he must have luck.[4]

However, these young National Servicemen learned to adapt to their surroundings with incredible dexterity. As more and more of them came to the battalion, the task of training them for jungle patrolling became more and more difficult and to add to this, the ever-growing reputation of the battalion saw many other individuals from the security forces now being pushed onto them for training in the 'art' of bandit-hunting. Joint police patrols were now becoming common.

Patrolling vast areas of secondary jungle – jungle that had already been reclaimed but had been allowed to revert to nature once more – was extremely difficult for an eight- to twelve-man patrol. Usually it would involve splitting the area into a grid and dividing each grid into smaller boxes of approximately 100 × 100 yards.

The idea was that the patrol could enter the jungle on a compass bearing and hack their way through to a distance of 100 yards, then stop and turn 90 degrees left and continue on for a further 100 yards, halt, do the same again and the same again. In theory if the lines were straight, then they would end up at the start position after four 'sweeps'. Reducing the distance would mean that the box being patrolled would become gradually smaller until its centre was reached. The principle was used extensively when good information was known about the specific location of a bandit camp.

As a rule, patrols generally kept off the tracks and paths in case they were ambushed. It was laborious and tedious work, but it had to be done. The average 'box' patrol would take three to four hours, with the leading scouts hacking most of the way with machetes and parangs. Progress was often slow, sometimes averaging just 50 yards an hour, as Second Lieutenant Robin Farmer recalled:

> The area we covered was almost entirely jungle, surrounded by rubber estates through which we had to pass before we reached the primary jungle. The worst part of the territory was the 'ulu' which was secondary jungle containing long sharp blades of grass which grew wild and gave no protection from sun or rain, both of which were in plentiful supply. We were also exposed in this type of ground as there was no cover. The rubber plantations were easier to patrol, and the trees were planted in meticulously straight rows, giving excellent visibility in a straight line but total cover in enfilade. We would typically patrol for three days at a time, sometimes longer, and would cover about 20 miles. Although we could make good progress in the rubber estates, patrolling the jungle was much

slower. A typical day was at about a half mile an hour through the undergrowth, having to hack our path through with machetes. Trying to be silent while doing this was a huge problem! We would rise at about 4 a.m. and drive to the point where we would patrol, aiming to be through the rubber estate and into the jungle before the curfew ended, which was 0600. It started again at 1400.[5]

Accurate maps of Malaya were virtually non-existent and often many years out of date. A map issued to Robin of the Tarun Estate in August 1952 was copied from a Victorian one, which was completely out of date as the land had already reverted to secondary jungle some twenty years earlier. When a good map could be obtained, the patrol commander guarded it fiercely and kept it away from the elements, usually folded neatly inside a flat metal 'Players' cigarette tin. The compass was essential in the jungle where it was impossible to distinguish any prominent landmarks.

Patrolling also had to cover the swampy areas of Malaya as well as the plantations and the jungles. This was tough going, as Private Tony Coote recalled:

> It goes without saying that this was not a pleasant experience. Most of the time we found ourselves up to the waist in water, muddy, foul-smelling water, with leeches that clung to your skin at any given opportunity. When you needed to sleep, you simply looked for a higher point and you climbed on and slept as best you could.[6]

Captain Arthur Campbell who commanded 'D' Company in 1950 recalled swamp patrolling and ambushes:

> You lay there on the edge of the swamp, belly-deep in water. As day follows night, you're attacked by the heat in the daytime, by the damp cold in the night-time, and by a million mosquitoes that settle on every exposed part of the body, and you can't move to brush them off because one movement can give your position away at a critical moment. Yet all this time you have to be vigilant, really vigilant, because when the enemy comes, he appears suddenly in front of you, and you have five seconds to despatch him, no more.[7]

The need for total silence when patrolling was essential. Men learned to communicate with one another by hand signals so that the element of surprise could be maintained. Second Lieutenant Pat Bird recalled their effectiveness:

> After a couple of hours, I received a sign passed along the line from the back that they had seen bandits. No one spoke, it was all done by signs, as we had rehearsed so often, and I saw two chaps coming towards us. They had not seen us, and as we were so quiet, had not heard us either. We all quietly took up firing positions, and the two bandits walked obliviously towards us.[8]

Ready in their pre-rehearsed ambush positions, Pat continued:

> I was just about to open fire when there was a shot from down the line, and I found later that the Iban tracker had not been able to contain himself, he was so keen to kill someone – they put little tattoos on their knuckles for all the people they claimed to have killed. Then everyone opened up and for about five seconds it was chaos. I called the patrol to cease fire, and to Corporal Chapman to take his half of the patrol round to the left while I went round to the right to see if we could see any other bandits and to find out about the two who must have been hit.[9]

Ibans had been with the battalion since early 1950. These men, who heralded from Sarawak in Borneo, were adept jungle fighters who knew how to live off the land and survive in the jungle. They could spot the very smallest signs of activity and could track an enemy by the minutest of traces that would go unnoticed by most eyes.

Their appearance was, at first, foreboding. Covered in tattoos and with long hair, they struck a sinister pose. The rumour went around that they were head-hunting cannibals and were paid based on the number of scalps they collected. Many a National Serviceman worried about being on stag duty at night with these men lest they were after his head!

However, soon their fears diminished as their loyalty was confirmed. The men soon started to catch on quickly to their skills of jungle survival. After being on patrol with them a couple of times, men instinctively became observant, scouring the jungle for signs of disturbance. They began to learn that a broken twig, a pushed back creeper or trodden grass could give clues as to the direction of a bandit party, and often the Iban could smell cigarette smoke or food being cooked deep in the undergrowth where others could not.

The High Commissioner himself had seen them on parade with the battalion and recommended the creation of two Iban platoons. The Suffolk section was brought up to strength with the addition of Dyak tribesmen, while another platoon was formed for use with the Scottish Rifles (Cameronians).

Now placed under the command of Lieutenant 'Bob' Godfrey, the Ibans' appearance was made slightly less foreboding with the issue of a jungle green uniform and a 'short back and sides'. All would later be presented with the General Service Medal for their part in assisting the battalion and such was their pride at being part of the regiment that many wore coloured regimental side caps in camp that they had made up specially by the regimental contractor.

The regimental contractor was an important part of a soldier's life, supplying him with essentials of cleaning and polishing as well as the small comforts of home. Khan M.A. Hamid had loyally served the battalion with his shop and canteen since they first arrived in Egypt in 1946. In addition to selling the usual 'Brasso' metal polish and

'Nugget' boot polish, he spoke five languages and his family had served as British army contractors since 1851.

He stocked a wide variety of items including lighters, clocks and shields bearing the regimental badge that could be sent home to parents and loved ones as Christmas presents. Perhaps not surprisingly, Yardley talcum powder was one of his best sellers; a necessity to reduce chafing on the nether regions when on sweaty patrols.

Quite often, his 'char-wallahs' would follow the men out to the edges of the jungle with their urns of tea and would be there waiting for them when they returned. He even obtained permission on one occasion to send his char-wallahs into the jungle by helicopter when the battalion was out on Operation ASBAB. He also ran a laundry service for the cleaning and starching of uniforms and for time off in town, he stocked a range of hideously wide 'American' ties.

Intelligence was now the key to success and from mid-1950 the Malay Special Branch had made great inroads into the local Chinese population and had started to cultivate a large network of undercover informers.

After every patrol an intelligence report was completed. It requested valuable information as to the intention of the patrol and its duration. It asked for information about the patrol's composition, its members, the weapons that they carried and the areas they covered. It also contained sections to be completed about bandits encountered and who fired first.

The information from these crucial reports assisted the police to see which areas contained abnormal bandit activity and which methods of patrolling were most effective. Soon data was collated to suggest that a patrol strength of eight to ten men was most effective, and those of one to two days' duration fostered the best results without exerting the army to the physical fatigue brought on by longer operations. Larger, longer operations as had been experienced in the first months of the Briggs' plan were shown to be ineffective and costly and needed large resources to resupply troops by air-drop.

A good example of the failure of such large-scale operations was Operation BLAST in April 1950. Many different units, including the RAF complete with a squadron of Lincoln bombers and a Sunderland flying boat, were to be involved. Artillery units were to pound the target area in conjunction with the battalion's mortar platoon. Yet despite many elaborate precautions, which included the battalion travelling to their debussing points in civilian lorries with police drivers in plain clothes, after much active patrolling virtually no enemy contact was made. Inevitably, with so much build-up of troops and equipment, the Min Yuen realized that an operation was imminent and informed the bandits in advance.

On 4 May the mortar platoon, operating as infantry alongside 'C' Company, killed five bandits and 'C' Company itself killed one. Four more were captured. On 9 May, 'C' Company in the Brookside rubber estate near Kajang killed three more bandits and recovered a large cache of arms and ammunition. That evening, 'D' Company killed four more bandits and more arms were recovered. The following morning, 12 Platoon, 'D' Company searched a tin mine and killed one more. In the space of a week following Operation BLAST, fourteen bandits had been eliminated from patrols launched at less than thirty minutes' notice from information received the same day. Decisiveness and speed were the main reasons for these successes.

From the outset, Briggs had sought to bring the army and the police together, usually in the same building, so that inter-force co-operation on operations became mandatory. Special Branch had a growing network of informers and spies within the Malayan Communist Party and guarded these fiercely from any army interference.

The crucial link between the police and their information network and the battalion was the Intelligence Section. 'I' Section worked in close co-operation with local planters and tappers, and with the police, to sift through information received into lines of enquiry for suitable operations and patrols.

Sometimes, though, their information could be most unreliable and in an effort to collate better data Captain Starling, who had become the battalion's intelligence officer, sometimes took to gathering intelligence himself, as Lance Corporal Len Spicer of the Intelligence Section recalled:

> In the early days of the Battalion's tour, most of the intelligence came through either the Federation Police or Special Branch. As time went on more and more bandits surrendered and led patrols back to find camps. These were known as 'SEPs' [Surrendered Enemy Personnel]. However, after the Battalion came back from Penang in December 1950 and took over operations in Selangor, there was much more incentive to gather our own intelligence, particularly when 'Joe' became I.O. at Kajang, prior to Ernie Morgan taking over full time. Joe was of the opinion that where possible we (that is members of the section) should be able to go out and get information which would be more reliable.[10]

Intelligence for the battalion covered a large area and was often divided into sub-areas with a tactical headquarters centred on the area of each operation. 'Central Circle', as it was known, was the entire area for which the battalion had responsibility.

The central headquarters was a building in the centre of Kuala Lumpur where an office was shared with the police. Into this office came much of the intelligence from informers and from the local population, which was jointly analyzed by the police and the intelligence officer with assistance from a sergeant, a corporal and two other ranks.

When information was received, an operation would be planned as far as possible based upon past experience and the availability of men. Quite often for expedience, the message would be sent direct to the duty company office, from where they would send out orders to mobilize the standby platoon immediately.

The duty company always had two platoons ready for 'immediate action' with men ready to move at ten minutes notice. Of platoon strength of approximately thirty men, quite often it would be segregated into two smaller patrols, with the platoon sergeant taking one patrol and the platoon commander taking the other.

Tactical Headquarters ('Tac HQ') was the nerve centre of any operation and it was usually here that the battalion commander and the relevant company commanders would congregate to hear news of a patrol's progress, often crowding around the telephone or the wireless set to hear the scheduled checks. One reporter noted its interior on a visit in 1951:

> One wall is covered with an elaborate diagram of the local communist organization, and photographs of many terrorists. The names of most of them and the formations they belong to are known. Thus the Suffolks do not fight an unknown enemy. About half of their successes were won because of information given by the local Chinese and the others by constant patrolling and intelligent reading of the situation. Every bit of information is followed up. Plans are ready in case an estate is attacked. On the wall beneath the situation charts hang maps with approach routes marked, and to them pinned operational orders.[11]

For those who worked there, it could be a rewarding job if contact was made and a bandit eliminated, and usually they were the first to know of a 'kill', but it could also be frustrating for those who wished to be out there on patrol having a crack at the enemy, but their job was equally important, even if they never felt so at the time.

In October 1950, news came that Captain Arthur Campbell had been gazetted with the Military Cross for his actions in Malaya. His platoon had accounted for more than twenty bandits killed and the citation for his award praised his meticulous and skilful planning of operations and his vigorousness and thorough actions that led to their continued success. He returned home shortly afterwards to accept a position at the Staff College at Camberley and started to write *Jungle Green*, a semi-fictionalized account of the battalion's campaign in Malaya. Published in 1953, it proved so popular that 15,000 copies were sold in the first three weeks after publication and it went on to be reprinted seven times. It was later serialized on radio both in the UK and in the US under the title of *Suspense*. In writing to Colonel Nicholson of the Suffolk Regiment about the success of his book, Campbell remarked:

> The real hero, of course, is the private soldier, without whose magnificent courage and endurance none of the things I describe could have been brought to pass. I am of course delighted that the people of the Empire are reading at first hand of what is going on in Malaya, and even more so, because they were collected under the name of our wonderful regiment.[12]

Patrolling continued day in and day out. When information was received, the 'Standby Platoon' was immediately mobilized into action. Here men of 4 Platoon – the 'platoon of the day' – get ready to go out again on a patrol. The men wait with their kit ready on the steps of the accommodation area at Kajang. Lance Corporal Bernie Philips can be seen in the background.

Within minutes, the patrol would be delivered to a spot close to the jungle's edge and would set off in pursuit. A member of 1 Platoon, 'A' Company is seen here in the thick lalang (elephant grass) and tall ferns. His comrade is barely visible just a few yards back.

A halt of 5 Platoon in a jungle clearing. The area appears to have been cleared of vegetation in the not-too-distant past, perhaps for a previous air-drop or helicopter landing, but it didn't take the jungle long to reclaim it. Dwarfed in the centre, Privates Wyant, Elmer and Crack smile for the camera.

A patrol of 8 Platoon, 'C' Company crosses a jungle stream or 'chaung'. Here a good view can be seen of a complete nine-man patrol in action. The photographer Private Ken Ambrose was the leading scout and the first man across, who paused to take this photograph. The fourth man back carries the EY rifle with its muzzle covered. Ken's officer, Second Lieutenant Mike Pensotti, is seventh in line, with the Bren-gunner behind.

'Mr Parry having breakfast.' Early morning in the jungle and Second Lieutenant David Parry is drinking tea. His aluminium drinking cup was modelled on American designs; its contoured shape was designed to allow it to fit snugly over the bottom of the water bottle when carried. He wears a thick woollen balaclava of a style sold by Jaeger and on his wrist he wears the standard ATP (Army Trade Pattern) watch, which had to be indented from battalion stores. In the background 'Ipoh', his Iban tracker, watches the photographer.

(**Above**) Using a twig for stirring, Lance Corporal Cooper of 6 Platoon, 'B' Company brews tea for himself and the section commander, Second Lieutenant Pat Bird, during a patrol out of Kuala Kubu Bharu. One of the mess tins resting on the fire is an old oval-shaped Indian-made variety as seen during the war in Burma.

(**Opposite, above**) Three other cheerful members of 6 Platoon brewing tea. They have slung a poncho cape up as some protection against the piercing sun. The cape had a small pocket on the inside designed to hold a tin of anti-gas ointment. It can just be seen here, along with a No. 5 Jungle Carbine in front of the camera.

(**Opposite, below**) No. 6 Platoon's two Iban trackers rest under their basha while dinner is being prepared. One of their distinctive long, native knives or parangs can be seen lying beside one of their packs, while lying in the background are more water bottles and mess tins.

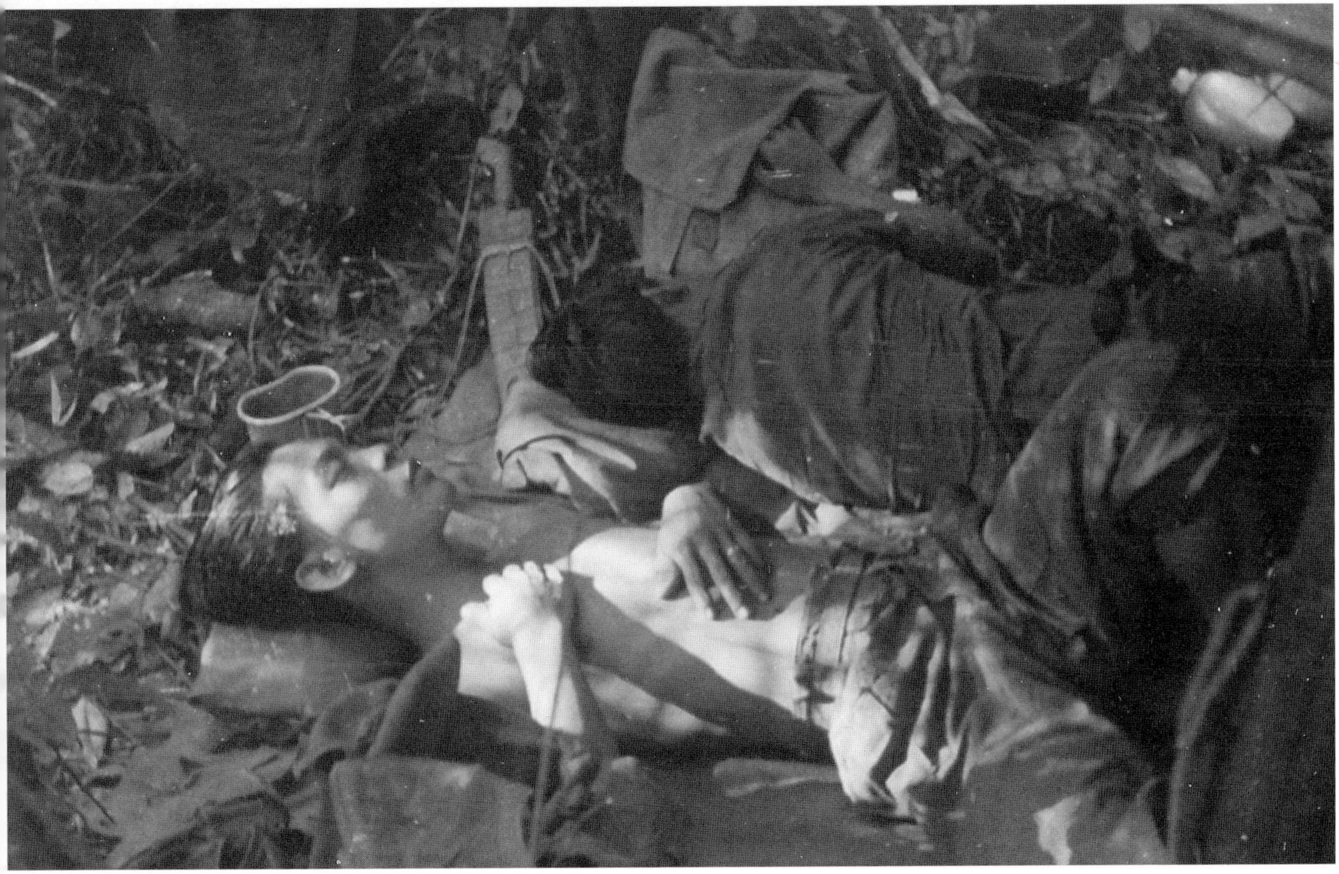

Patrolling a rubber plantation and a halt for a drink. The man in the foreground, whose wireless set sits to his right, is parting the cup from the bottom of his water bottle. Around his neck he wears a white cotton 'sweat rag'; most probably a hand towel purchased in one of the numerous shops dotted around their camp.

A watched kettle never boils. Here men of 'B' Company wait expectantly for a cup of tea being brewed over a jungle fire. It must have been close to the end of a long patrol as their exhaustion is evident. Standing with a cigarette in hand is Lieutenant Arnold Palmer, who later commanded the regiment's contingent at the Coronation Parade in London in 1953.

Two men of 1 Platoon brew up tea using their small portable stoves during a halt while patrolling the New Caledonia rubber estate. A good view can be seen of the 1944 Pattern equipment braces, which contained four straps across the back. Its wider shoulder pads helped spread the weight more effectively, but in reality they were seldom worn. The man sitting on the left has a block of compressed freeze-dried tea ready to drop into his mess tin when the water boils.

(**Opposite, above**) A jungle camp created by 6 Platoon, 'B' Company with its radio-operator and guard staying behind while the remainder are out on patrol. With his headphones on, the set's operator listens out for orders for the patrol from camp. The radio's antenna appears to be coiled up the tree in the centre.

(**Above**) A good view of the neatness of the planting in the rubber plantations. In rows, it was relatively easy to spot a bandit between the trees and fire could be brought upon him. If a bandit was seen passing diagonally, then the trees gave him almost total cover.

(**Opposite, below**) A tired but happy patrol of 6 Platoon, 'B' Company awaits their transport back to base. Private Ron Newlands, seated left, appears to be eating half a coconut, the other half of which is perhaps being scooped out by his colleague standing right, who uses his bayonet for the task. Note the distinctive diamond-pattern on the soft sole of the the jungle boots. Bandits' boots or 'bumpers' usually had ribbed soles and so it was relatively easy for the trackers to spot whether any footprints discovered were friend or foe.

Bandit Has Outlawed Suffolks

'BEARDED WONDER' LOSES 101 MEN

From Daily Mail Reporter

SINGAPORE, Tuesday.

OFFICERS and men of the 1st Bn. Suffolk Regt. in Malaya have had prices put on their heads by Chinese Communist Liew Kon-kim.

Liew is the bandit leader in Kajang, 17 miles from Kuala Lumpur.

He is known to our troops as "the bearded wonder," because he is the only bearded Chinese in the whole bandit corps.

The Suffolks earned the distinction of Liew's "outlaw" money offer through killing a record 101 bandits since their arrival in Malaya 20 months ago.

THE HARD WAY

One patrol shot and killed Raja Gopal, a leading Indian guerilla chief for whom authorities were offering a £1,200 reward. But no

(**Opposite, above**) A happy patrol of 4 Platoon, 'B' Company is captured making their way back to camp after an uneventful patrol. The old and battered Dodge weapons carriers were popular vehicles and were the most comfortable to travel in. Sitting in the foreground smiling is Private Brian Allen, who later left a substantial legacy to the Suffolk Regiment Museum.

(**Opposite, below**) Returning to base after a night patrol, the exhaustion is clearly evident on the faces of these men of 2 Platoon, 'A' Company. This photograph was taken on 26 June 1951 after they had been out on a night patrol to a deserted rubber factory near Ulu Klang. They had lain in ambush all night, but no bandits came as intelligence had suggested they would.

(**Above**) After alighting from the trucks, the men form up to be inspected by the patrol commander. The sign at the main gate to Wardieburn Camp featured a Suffolk Castle with the dates 1685 to 1949. As each year passed, the latter date was amended. Here it is in 1951.

(**Left**) The press made much of the 100th bandit killed by the battalion. It was Second Lieutenant Bob Godfrey who claimed the honour of making

the first 'century' for the Battalion. Bob, who joined the battalion from Sandhurst, was once described by a reporter as 'that type of Englishman who lives in an igloo in Greenland or crosses the Atlantic in a small sailing boat just for the sheer joy of it.' Bob later wrote the final volume of Regimental History covering the Malayan Emergency.

(**Above**) Tented accommodation at Kajang. Here, each platoon had its own tent slung over a steel frame and tied down to a wooden frame, which ran around its edges. The floor was made of concrete slabs and electric light was provided. Towels and socks can be seen slung over the guy ropes to dry.

(**Opposite, above**) 'D' Company's accommodation area at Wardieburn Camp. The huts were of 'Indian' style of attap leaves over a steel frame. In one tropical downpour in 1951, 5 Platoon's hut completely collapsed and although there were no casualties, it took days to clear the wreckage and recover all their bedding and personal belongings.

(**Opposite, below**) A man's bed space was his own sanctuary, even though it gave him very little privacy. Here Private Richard Baldwin of 'B' Company snapped his corner of the platoon tent with his few personal possessions. An old supply crate covered in a towel, with his alarm clock and a few photos of his family were all he had to remind him of home.

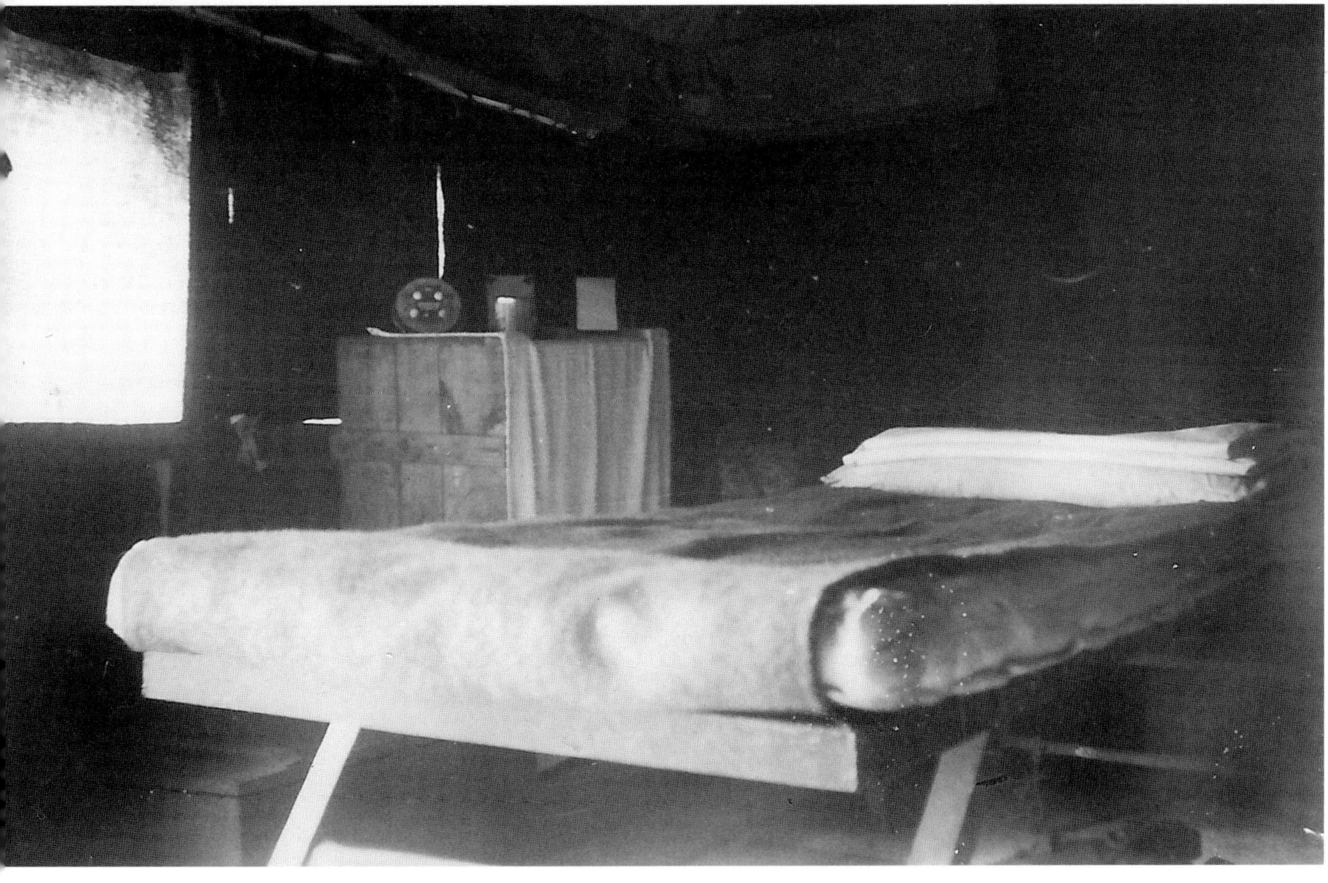

A view of the Support Company's tent with the sides rolled up for ventilation. Lying on his bed, Private Tony Gould reads a book. He has managed to obtain an old ration crate, which he is using as a bedside locker. Above his head hangs his machete and jungle hat, while further down the tent is a suit of woollen battledress. On the bed space in the foreground the local 'dhobi wallah' looks to have delivered its occupant his freshly-laundered clothing.

Sitting on his bed, Private Ted Monk writes a letter home. Ted lived in Baldock all his life and was an ardent supporter of the Hemel Hempstead branch of the Old Comrades Association.

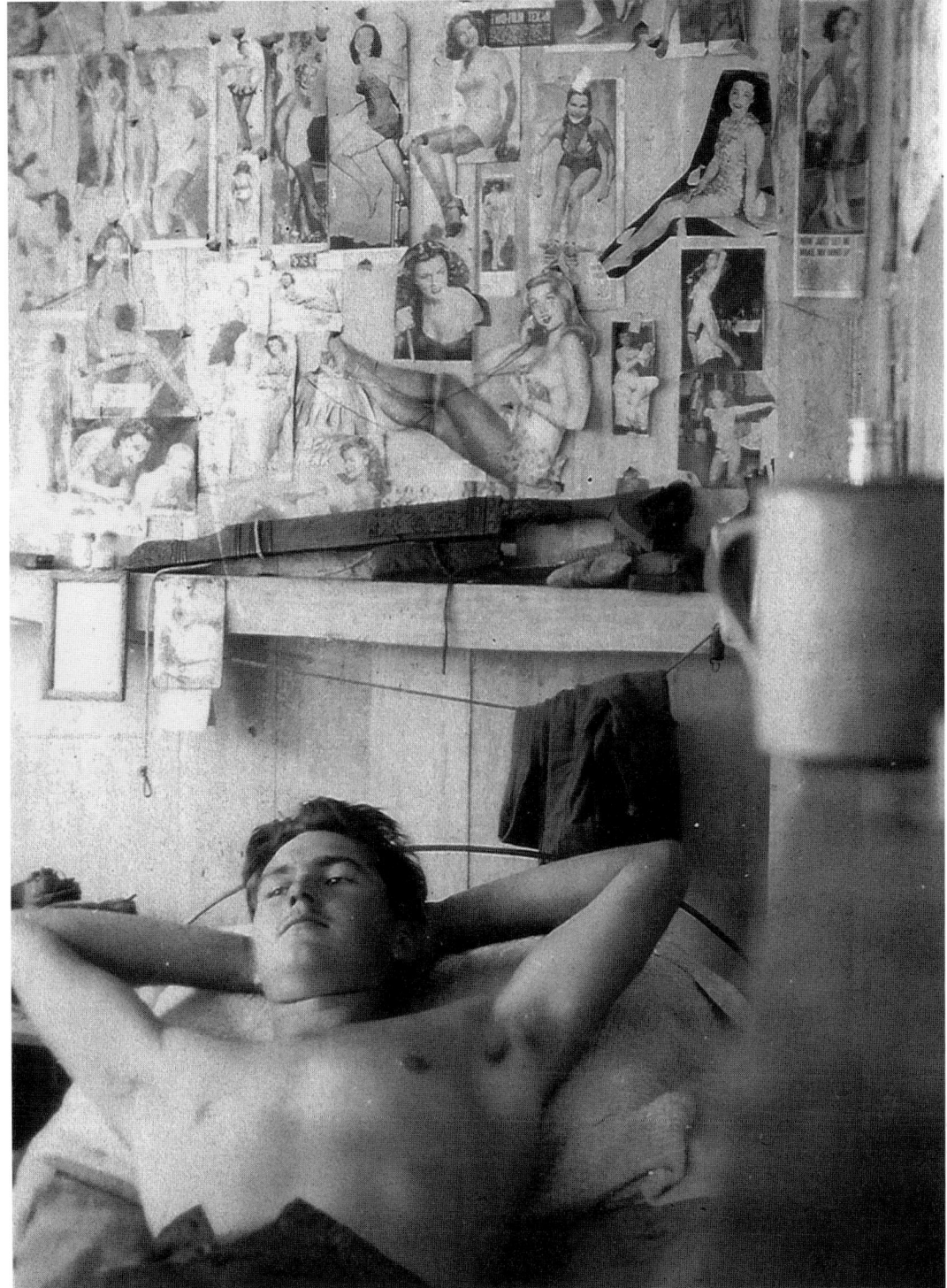

While on operations in 1950, 'A' Company was based at Sekamat where they had the 'luxury' of using a rubber tappers' accommodation block. Here a member of 1 Platoon is photographed with a corner of 'lovelies'. A native parang knife lies above his head on the shelf.

In between the important business of bandit-hunting, the age-old custom of 'bull' continued. Here a member of 5 Platoon polishes his ammunition boots for an imminent parade. The men also had to ensure that their belts and gaiters were freshly blancoed, which involved adding a paste of powdered web renovator onto the webbing, allowing it to dry and then brushing it off. Everyone hated doing it for the khaki dust got everywhere.

A reason for some celebration. Here men of 2 Platoon share a few 'Tigers' in their tent with the son of a local tradesman (who perhaps provided the cigars?). The man in the centre is a member of the Mortar Platoon, as can be seen by the patch on his jungle hat. Hanging on the right, a woollen battledress blouse can be seen with the patch of the 18th Independent Infantry Brigade and the regiment's distinctive 'Minden Flash' of red and yellow below it.

The label of the famous local Tiger Beer. Note the 'N.A.A.F.I. Stores, H.M. Forces' additions to their standard label. Another popular drink was 'Anchor' ABC Lager.

An unknown lance corporal drinks from a coconut outside the corporals' mess at Kajang. The mess was a tent named 'The Crooked Billet', which featured an entranceway of two black and white striped poles with the heads of two bandits in their distinctive pointed caps (seen here either side of the flap). A sign above proclaimed 'Drink Brown Ale!'

(**Right**) 'Lou Lou', the MT Section's pet monkey, is seen here taking a drink from a soldier's aluminium cup while Private Ted Monk looks on in amusement.

(**Below, left**) A joyous day when the mail finally arrived from home. Here, after months of delays and confusions, Lance Corporal Bernie Philips finally receives his letters from home. In 4 Platoon there were three 'Philips' and routinely the mail was incorrectly distributed.

(**Below, right**) It was not uncommon for parents at home to send out newspapers to their sons in Malaya to keep them up to date with local news. Private Bernie Elmer reads a copy of the *Yarmouth Mercury* that his mother sent out to him in early 1952. It seems that the sports news of his local team 'The Bloaters' was most interesting!

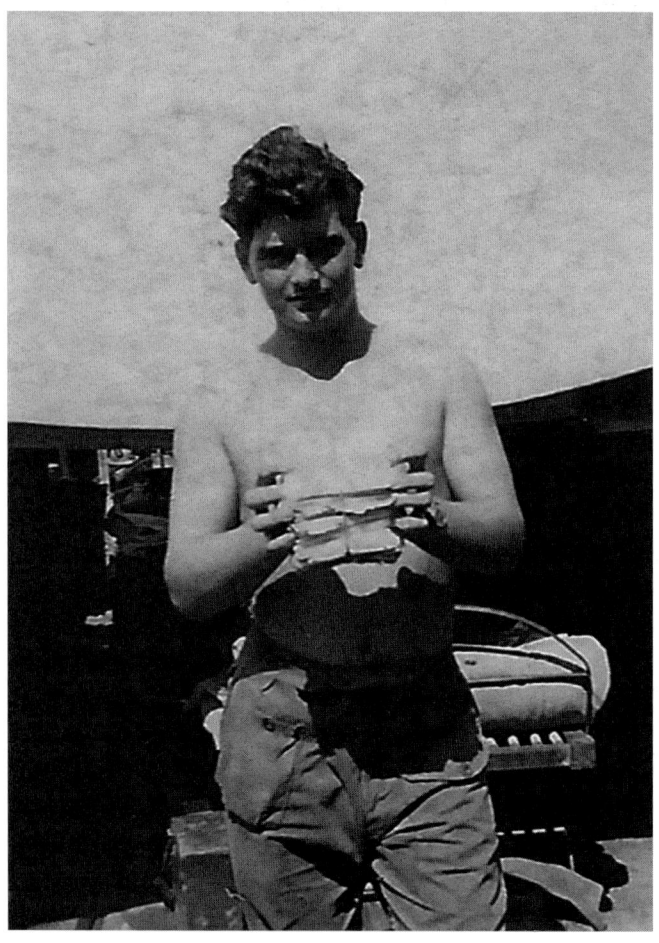

A similar scene with Private Fred Mullinder, right, of 4 Platoon, who reads the *Lowestoft Journal and Mercury* with his friend John Culley. Fred and John were called up together and served in 4 Platoon for their time in Malaya. They remained lifelong friends until John's death in 2015.

Fred's mother sent a virtually identical photograph to the newspaper who later published it.

Camp life at Wardieburn. After having his icebox checked, the local ice cream seller cycled around the camp selling ices to many an overheated soldier who needed cooling. Here, Corporal Fentiman of 'A' Company puts in his order.

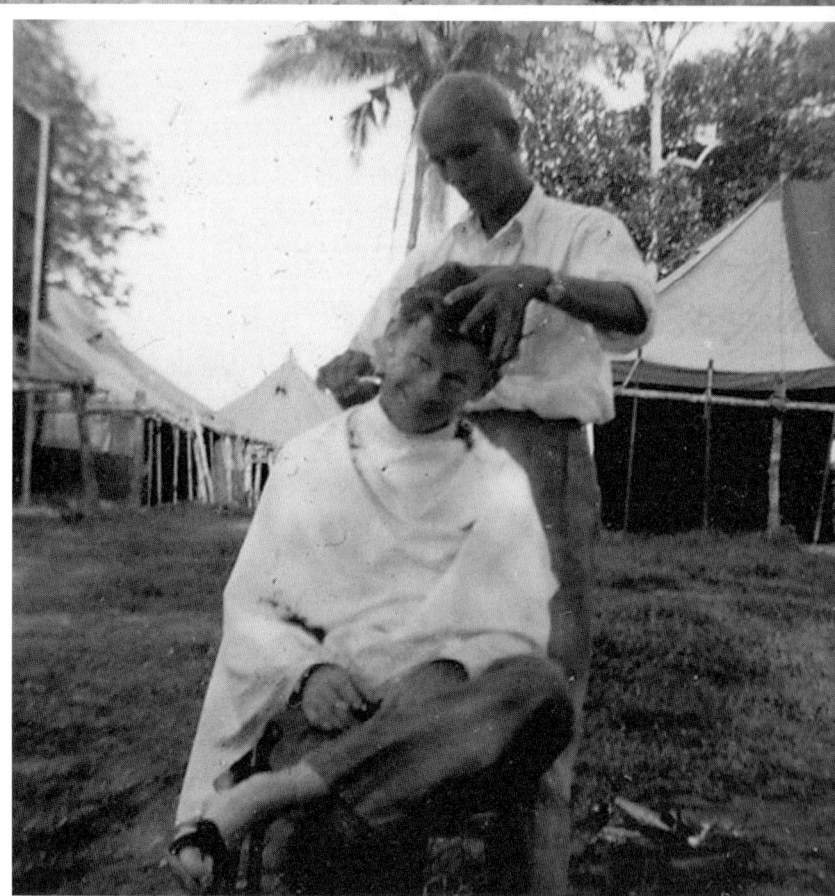

The local 'nappi' or barber would also visit the camp regularly to cut the men's hair. Here Corporal McHugh, the pay corporal, has his second haircut of the day 'because Sergeant Major Colleen wasn't satisfied!' The army owned everything just above the ear downwards. On top, anything that could be covered by a beret or a jungle hat was the soldier's own.

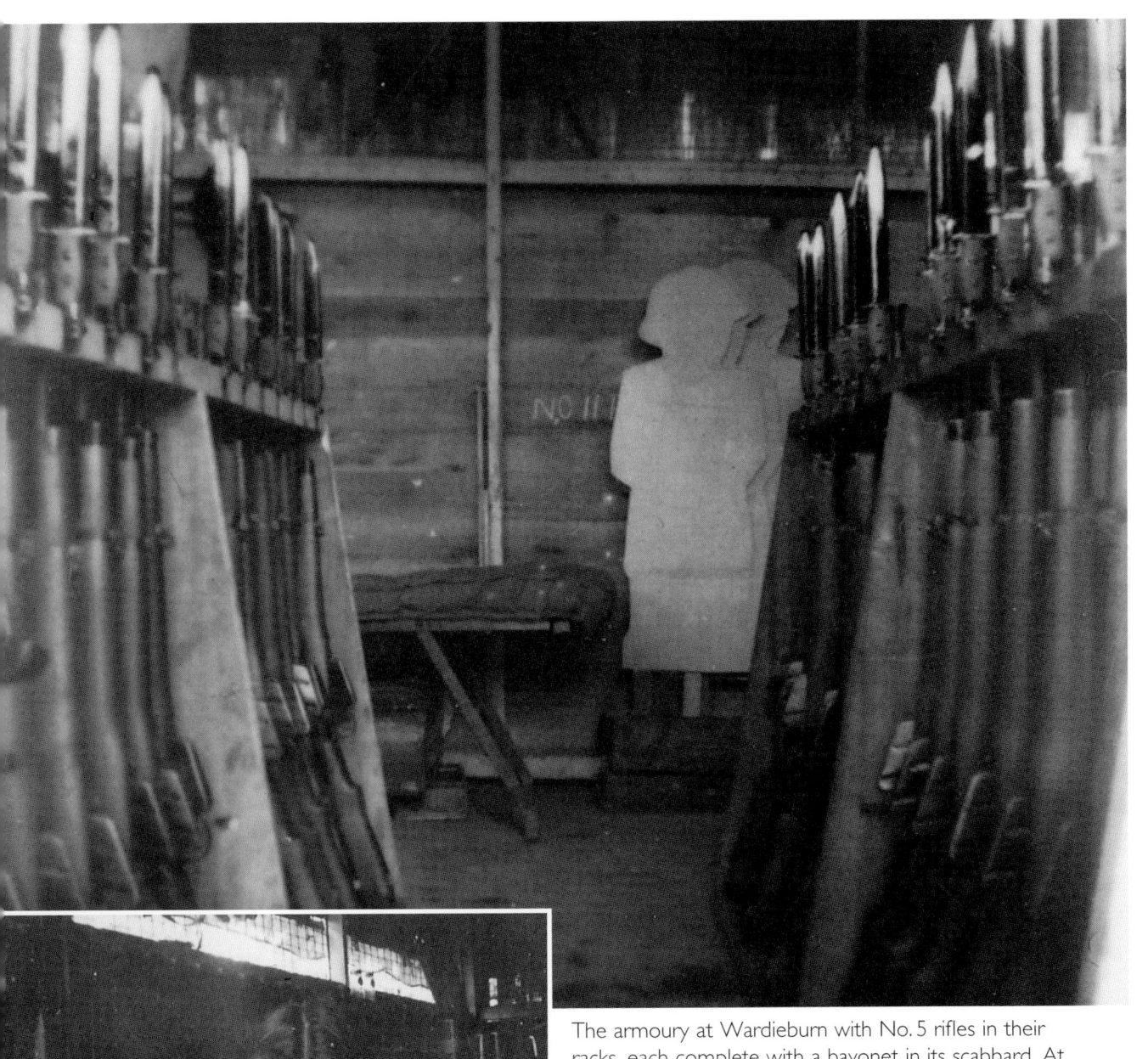

The armoury at Wardieburn with No. 5 rifles in their racks, each complete with a bayonet in its scabbard. At the back can be seen cut-out targets for practice and two crates of either No. 36 rifle grenades or No. 83 smoke grenades. At night the rifles were chained up and the senior private or the duty corporal slept in the armoury on the bunk at the back.

Seen here inside the armoury applying a coat of 'Japlac' black enamel paint to the scabbard of a No. 5 bayonet is Private Ross. Ross was an accomplished artist and was responsible for the battle honours on the battalion's vehicles, many platoon signs and the labelling of many a soldier's suitcase for his journey home.

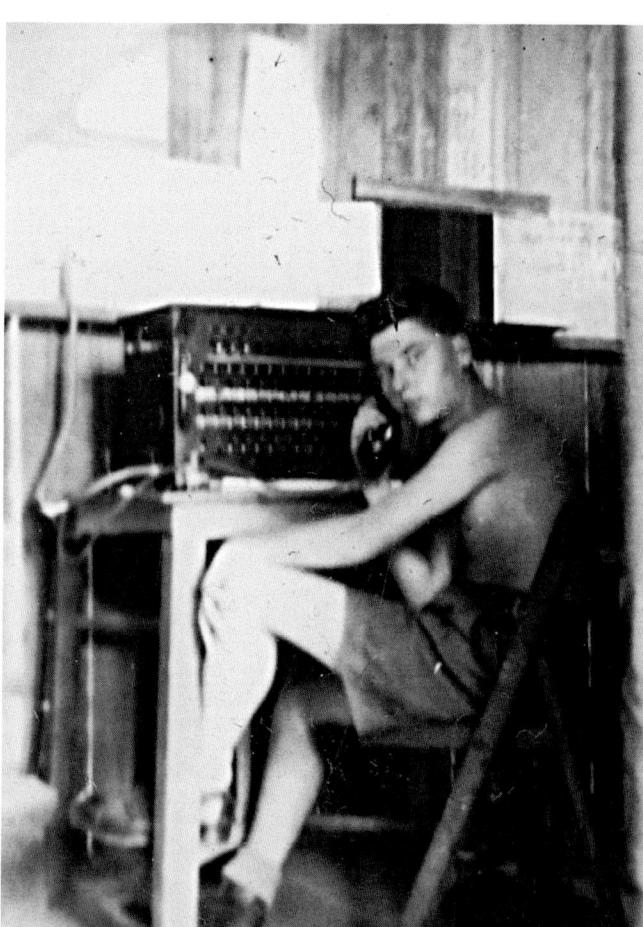

(**Opposite, above left**) Straight from the football field and still with his boots on, a member of the Standby Platoon goes to draw his Owen gun for operations from Private Brundish, who stands behind the armoury counter. The sign on the door proclaimed that 'All arms will be drawn by 1900 hrs.'

(**Opposite, above right**) The telephone exchange at Wardieburn; a vital link between the battalion and the outside world. The switchboard operator is seen here sitting in a small room beside the orderly room. From here, the battalion commander and the intelligence officer would receive orders to mobilize men for immediate action.

(**Opposite, below**) The NAAFI (Navy, Army and Air Force Institutes) club at Wardieburn. Here in a Nissen hut, the men could sit in comfy chairs and write letters to loved ones with a little more privacy than in their platoon tent. A small lending library was available from the bookcase at the rear.

(**Above**) For those who required guidance of the spiritual kind, a small makeshift outdoor chapel was established. The altar was an army-issue trestle table, covered here with the battalion flag of a red castle and key, on a yellow background below which was the numeral XII. An altar backdrop of a suspended grey army blanket is covered with Haig Fund poppies in preparation for a Remembrance Day service.

(**Above**) Another view of the chapel showing chairs borrowed from the officers' mess and the NAAFI for the service. These were placed in front for officers, and behind folding benches were laid out for NCOs and other ranks who wished to attend.

(**Opposite, above left**) Remembrance Day 1950. Privates Smith and Dawes of 10 Platoon, 'D' Company prepare to take the collection tin and a box of Haig Fund poppies to each tent to obtain donations for the British Legion.

(**Opposite, below**) Most men liked to pose for a photograph wearing a captured bandit cap. Here Private Clifton of 3 Platoon, 'A' Company poses outside his hut for a photograph to send home to his parents.

(**Opposite, above right**) Private Hurlock of 5 Platoon poses bare-chested at Sungei Manggis in early 1952. His jungle hat bears the distinctive shield of 'B' Company and its brim carries the label '5 PLN'.

Off-duty recreation at Kajang included table tennis. Private Brian Allen shows his prowess at the sport. The battalion had an active table tennis league, which published its leader board in the regimental magazine, the *Castle & Key*.

The 6-pounder anti-tank guns of the Support Company seen here in the gun park at Wardieburn. In reality, they were seldom used on operations and often only fired salutes when special visitors came to camp.

A view from the officers' mess over the central courtyard at Kajang. Seen here are many battalion vehicles including the water cart. A badminton court appears to have been marked out on the concrete slabs in the foreground.

(**Above**) Practice makes perfect. Men of 8 Platoon (which included left- and right-handed Owen-gunners) practise on the 30-yard range at Kajang. The man in the foreground wears a pair of black and white canvas and rubber 'hockey' boots and carries the distinctive pouch that held three magazines for his Owen gun.

(**Opposite, above**) Others practise with Bren guns, lying in the prone position. The man standing in the foreground with his hand on his hip wears a home-made pouch that contains four magazines for the M2 carbine, noticeable from their curved shape.

(**Opposite, below**) The same men now fire their Brens from the hip. The local boys watch from the safety of the tree on the right.

A display of bandit weapons for the benefit of the cameraman. These include a much-modified M1928 Thompson sub-machine gun, an old single-barrelled shotgun and a No. 4 rifle. Note the castle patches worn on their jungle hats. From left to right: Privates James Murray, Donald Fallan, Gordon Abbot and Ronald Baggatt.

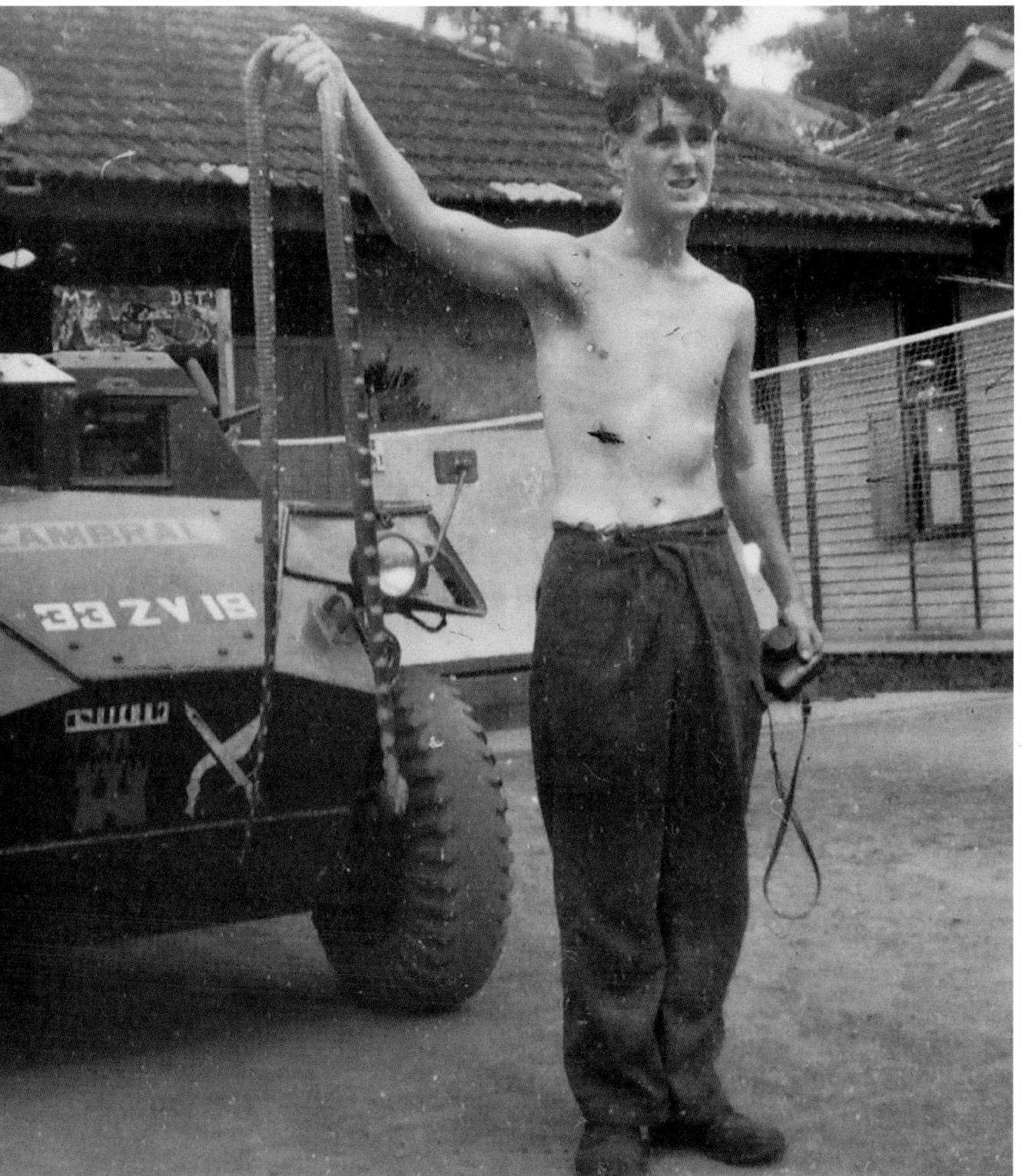

Camp may have been relatively safe from the bandits, but the local wildlife could not always be kept at bay. Here Private Derek Hexter, then serving in the MT Section, holds up a snake found in a scout car one morning. Note the battle honour 'Cambrai' on the scout car behind and the badminton net strung up for a game.

(**Opposite, above**) Two Ibans of 3 Platoon with their distinctive tattoos and long hair. Later their sinister appearance was calmed with a 'short-back-and-sides' haircut, although most men marvelled at how quickly the Ibans could tie up their hair into a bun and tuck it under their jungle hats.

(**Opposite, below**) A view of their backs with freshly-applied tattoos. Private George Flory, who took these photographs, noted how it was done: 'No electric needle, just a spike in a piece of wood. This is laid crossways over another piece of wood operated by the tattooist by hammering the wood with the needle into his mate's back.'

(**Above**) Two Dyak tribesmen photographed by Private John Hopkins in 1950. It was said that when an Iban or a Dyak got a kill, he added another tattoo.

(**Opposite, above, left**) 'Chico' and 'Banyan', 12 Platoon's two Iban trackers. Such was their loyalty to the regiment that, as seen here, they were permitted to wear Suffolk cap badges and Chico has even had a regimental side cap of dark blue cloth with a yellow peak made up specially by the battalion contractor. It was said that their wristwatches were taken from the bodies of dead terrorists. (**Right**) Two more Ibans of 'D' Company. These two men come from the same Borneo tribe and sport matching tattoos on their throats. Both are armed with the No. 4 rifle. Seldom were the trackers given anything else to carry when on patrol.

(**Opposite, below**) In its early days of patrolling, a contingent of Fijians was brought in to assist the battalion on operations. They were nicknamed 'Wuzzies' and were extremely proud of the accolade given to them. They were superb trackers and unlike the Ibans, they drank copious amounts of tea like the British.

(**Above**) Under the guard of Lieutenant Tony Cobbold (inset), the Colours of the 1st Battalion are paraded at Kajang in 1951. Presented in 1849, they were the oldest Colours still to be carried by any regiment in the British army when they were finally retired in 1955. Shortly after this photograph was taken, they were sent to Singapore to be placed in cold storage before their already fragile silk fell apart in the humid climate of Malaya.

(**Opposite, above**) Farewell to the outgoing battalion commander, Lieutenant Colonel Ian Wight. Men of 4 Platoon, just back from patrol, parade in their jungle boots and hats, while 5 Platoon parade in starched jungle greens, scrubbed webbing and ammo boots. Most men here wear the older style of wartime GS cap and khaki berets. Later, men arriving from England wore the 'midnight blue' beret issued to all National Servicemen on joining the regiment. Lieutenant Colonel Wight was later promoted to brigadier and awarded the Distinguished Service Order for his command of the battalion in Malaya. He was later sent on a lecture tour in the US to speak on British actions in the Far East.

(**Opposite, below**) A photo call for an American journalist to see what weapons an average patrol carried. Here at Wardieburn, men of 'B' and 'D' companies are paraded with their arms: an Owen submachine gun, an EY rifle, a No. 5 jungle carbine, a Bren gun and an M2 carbine. Private Fred Mullinder carries the Bren and to his left, Sergeant Peck carries the M2 carbine.

(**Above**) A dummy with captured bandit uniform and equipment is supported by two members of 'D' Company. The dummy was later sent home to be displayed in the Regimental Museum where it can still be seen today.

'The gun-carrying carol singers of Malaya.' Men of 5 Platoon sing carols to a planter and his family on the Tuan Mee Estate on Christmas Eve 1951. The scout car in the background bears the battle honour of 'Macedonia', while holding the torch in the foreground is Second Lieutenant Ray Hands. Sergeant Albert Tracey holds the lantern in the centre, whilst standing left looking drenched is Private Raymond 'Pedlar' Palmer.

'Pedlar' was quite a character at regimental reunions playing the spoons and being able into his 70s to recite all verses of 'We haven't seen Liew Kon Kim for a helluva time'. In 1977 he was awarded the Royal Humane Society Bronze Medal for rescuing a fellow fisherman when their trawler capsized off the Cornish coast. Pedlar gave his life-jacket to his colleague and pulled him into a life raft. Only he and two others survived the sinking. Here his tattoo of a clipper in sail can be seen on his chest.

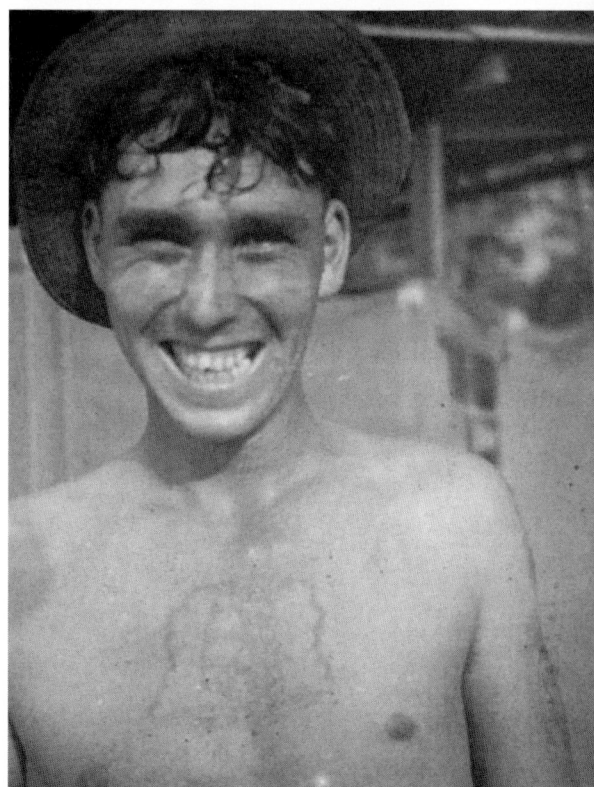

After their musical efforts, the platoon was invited in for drinks. Drenched from a tropical downpour, they all share a beer with the planter and his family. Standing fourth from right is 'B' Company's commander Major Malcolm Dewar with a beer in hand. Dewar was related in a small way to the highland whisky distillers and was known affectionately by his junior subalterns as the 'Monarch of the Ulu' in homage to Landseer's famous painting 'Monarch of the Glen'. Shy of the publicity, Second Lieutenant Ray Hands stands quietly at the back.

Getting ready for a night on the town, this member of 9 Platoon laces up his 'bumpers' ready to board the truck into Kuala Lumpur. The battalion recognized that it was important with aggressive, continual patrolling to give the men regular downtime to relax. Usually one night a month was allocated to sending small groups into town to 'let off steam'.

Waiting for transport into Klang, Private Perry of 4 Platoon talks with Private Ted Philips who was just going out on patrol. Philips was a professional footballer for Leiston Town before he was called up for National Service, later signing for Ipswich Town with whom he had a highly successful career for more than ten years. His brother 'Lucky' Philips also served with the battalion as did Bernie 'Phil' Philips, so there was always a fair amount of confusion when the mail arrived!

The Boston Photographic Studios in Kuala Lumpur where many a soldier could have his portrait taken to send home. On its roof, the advertising slogan 'Time for a Tiger' can be seen.

A humorous photo most probably taken in their studios featuring Private Prothero of 1 Platoon in a jockey's cap and riding a toy horse. His khaki serge GS cap is seen perched on the horse's head.

No. 5 Platoon on a visit to the Snake Temple in Penang. Some men are in civilian dress and others in jungle greens, but all men are armed. American T-shirts and bowling shirts were very popular when off duty such as those worn by Private Blick, left, and Private Baggot, fourth from left.

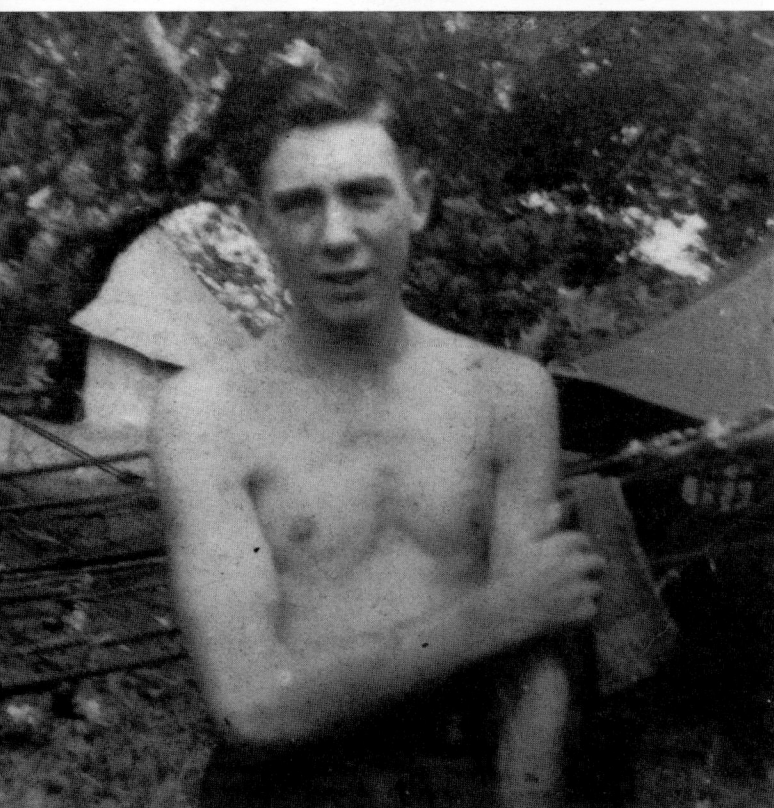

After much haggling with the locals, Private Mike Gilbert, left, appears to have struck a deal for his chums to obtain pineapples and bananas. The men all wear black-on-khaki 'slip-on' shoulder titles on their epaulettes, a badge that disappeared from use in 1940–41 with the introduction of cloth shoulder titles but seems to have been widely reissued for wear on jungle greens in Malaya.

Back from town and getting ready once again to go out on patrol. Private John Bye of 3 Platoon, 'A' Company, is photographed at Kajang in 1951. John was the chairman of the Leiston Branch of the Old Comrades Association and together with his wife, Anne, they organized many of the branches' social events and functions. He did much to keep alive the spirit of the Suffolk Regiment in East Suffolk.

Chapter Four

'The Best in Their Field'

The late spring of 1951 saw the bandits turning their attention to the telephone wires, a lifeline between the battalion, the outlying police stations and the plantation owners. On 10 May the wires were cut in the Banting area and a patrol of 'A' Company was sent to investigate.

The following day, a patrol of 8 Platoon, 'C' Company under the command of Sergeant 'Dilly' Wright was patrolling the jungle near Bukit Tekala when they met a sizeable group of bandits. Moving through an overgrown rubber plantation as they descended a hill in single file, they were ambushed from above.

Private Lionel Killick, who was leading scout, was hit along with the Bren-gunner and his No. 2 behind. In an exposed position Sergeant Wright, who had also been hit and was bleeding badly, now shouted to Lance Corporal Price to take over.

Being some 20 yards from the nearest man and realizing quickly that he was greatly outnumbered by the enemy, Price called to the four unwounded members of the patrol to hold their positions and return fire. Armed with a jungle carbine, Price fired up at the bandits on the ridge, killing two and wounding at least two others. Ordering the signaller to make contact with base to request immediate assistance, Price now took the EY rifle from the nearest wounded man and alone, he fired off a series of grenades at the enemy along the ridge.

For more than an hour the patrol returned fire and repulsed a separate attack made at them from along the track. Under fire, Price now ran over to the signaller to help him for the wireless set was now not working, the patrol being just out of range. Despite repeated efforts, Price now ordered the set's redundant operator, Private 'Daddy' Knight, to take Sergeant Wright's compass and run the gauntlet of fire through the position and out to the road for assistance. Making it through, Knight commandeered the first car that came along and ordered its driver to take him to the nearest police station where he telephoned to HQ for assistance.

Meanwhile, Price was still busy, running around under fire seeing to the wounded and making sure that their perimeter was held around the hill. After a further half an hour, with their ammunition expended, the bandits finally withdrew. There were now four members of the twelve-man patrol wounded, and everyone hoped that Private Knight had made it through for help.

Back at camp, even before Knight's message came through, reports were coming in of intense small-arms fire in the jungle at Bukit Tekala and CSM Keeble had already been ordered to take a detachment out immediately to assist. As he herded men into two trucks that were waiting, many were still getting their kit and jungle boots on as it sped away. Soon it stopped on the edge of the jungle where distant firing could be heard as the men formed up and set off. Private Ernie Guest, another member of 8 Platoon, was a member of that party and recalled the day:

> Distant firing could still be heard as we entered the overgrown rubber at the run, escorting a medical team. It must have been nearly an hour before we reached the scene and during that time the firing had died out. We joined the survivors in a close defensive ring around the wounded while other platoons occupied the higher ground further out. Sgt Wright was badly wounded but was quickly evacuated, but Private Lionel Killick was in a very bad way and it took the medics some time to stabilise him before he could be evacuated. Two others were wounded, Private Ellis in the wrist, and Private Chambers in the knee. This was from a section of only ten men with two Iban trackers. They had fought off a bandit force estimated at least 30 strong.[1]

The following day Private Lionel Killick died of his injuries in hospital. Bill Price, a young National Serviceman, was later awarded the Distinguished Conduct Medal, the last to be awarded to a soldier of the Suffolk Regiment. His citation noted that 'There is no doubt that the actions of L/Cpl Price were responsible for turning what might have been a serious disaster into a considerable success.' When he returned home to be demobbed, the mayor of Hornchurch in Essex where Price lived gave a celebration street party in his honour.

On 21 August 1951, the battalion officially accounted for its 100th bandit. Another patrol of 8 Platoon led by Lieutenant Bob Godfrey was 'bumped' by a party of bandits. Opening fire immediately, the patrol accounted for two bandits at some considerable distance. Two others fled. Such was this milestone of achievement that the Selangor Club held a dinner for the battalion's officers in honour of the occasion and presented them with a specially-commissioned drape for one of its music stands with 'Selangor Club 1951' embroidered under the regimental crest.

Now, using both the *Suffolk Regimental Gazette* published quarterly at home and the battalion's in-house magazine, the *Castle & Key*, published fortnightly in Malaya, the new battalion commander, Lieutenant Colonel Philip Morcombe, actively promoted the rivalry between platoons.

The *C&K* was typed and copied in battalion HQ office. It was usually eight pages of double-sided type, with a carbon-copied front cover depicting two soldiers of the regiment in the uniforms of 1685 and the 1950s, either side of a castle's portcullis and drawbridge. It was drawn by Private Deaves of 'A' Company HQ.

It contained occasional notes from the officers', sergeants' and the corporals' messes and was primarily a light-hearted dig at the monotonous patrols and mishaps in camp, but perhaps most importantly, it kept a running total of company scores and as the 100 mark was passed, all became fiercely competitive in trying to make their platoon top of the leader board. It was an important tool in keeping up morale in the battalion when it was averaging one 'kill' or contact for every six patrols mounted.

Trying to keep up enthusiasm in the ranks for active patrolling was of paramount importance and inter-company rivalry was a clever way of ensuring that men wanted to go out and get another kill to put their company in front on the scoreboard.

In July 1951, RSM Windley left and was replaced by RSM Duffy. Kevin Duffy was no stranger to the heat or the jungle. He joined the 2nd Suffolks in 1933 and served with them in the Arakan and at Imphal during the war. A broad Irishman, his imposing moustache was remembered by many a National Serviceman, together with the mischievous twinkle in his eye.

With a dispersed battalion, the role of RSM was difficult and rarely did the entire battalion assemble as a complete unit. He would often jibe many a young soldier for the quality of their jungle shaving when back off patrol, knowing full well that the job they were doing was first-class and that if he could, he would be out there with them.

Just as the security forces thought they were finally turning the tide, a major setback came with the death of the British High Commissioner, Sir Henry Gurney. On 6 October 1951, Gurney had been travelling in his car to Fraser's Hill when he was ambushed. Though the battalion's operational area was some miles away, they were placed on an immediate alert to set off in pursuit of his killers. The call never came and the following day, RSM Duffy was given the solemn task of preparing a Guard of Honour for his funeral.

Christmas 1951 saw some men of the battalion being invited for drinks at a local planter's bungalow. 'B' Company turned up at the Tuan Mee Estate on Christmas Eve to sing carols to its owner and in the New Year a photograph appeared in the *Illustrated London News* showing the 'Gun-carrying carol singers of Malaya'. All looked rather wet, having driven through a late-night downpour to get there, but their carols by torchlight were much appreciated.

News of the battalion's increasing success was now reaching far and wide. They were being visited regularly by dignitaries, officials and government ministers to see how the battle against communism was being fought. Though the Emergency lacked the glamour of the media-eclipsing United Nations war in Korea, it was nonetheless slowly gaining momentum in its success. Lieutenant Bob Godfrey recalled:

> 1951 had been a very successful year for the Battalion and its reputation in Malaya was already extremely high … newspapers and magazines were constantly seeking interviews with officers and men and much publicity was given to the Battalion's exploits in the UK press. 'Cassandra' of the *Daily Mirror* went on

patrol with a B Company platoon and wrote about his experiences in the *Daily Mirror* on 22 December 1951, and *The Times* devoted a full two columns to the Battalion in March 1952. Meanwhile earlier, Harry Hopkins wrote lengthy articles about the Battalion in two consecutive editions of 'John Bull', which was at the time a mass circulation weekly in the United Kingdom.[2]

Shortly after Lieutenant General Sir Harold Briggs left Malaya, in December 1951 the Secretary of State for the Colonies, the Rt Hon Oliver Lyttelton visited 'A' Coy at Kajang and was presented to a fighting patrol just back from the jungle. Second Lieutenant Mike Benn, an officer of the Royal Army Ordnance Corps on detachment to the battalion, was paraded with his men and their Iban tracker, much to the interest of Mr Lyttelton, who was later presented with a bandit cap by Second Lieutenant Mike Casey as a souvenir of his visit, its former owner 'having ceased to have any further need of a hat of any kind a few days earlier'.[3]

Lyttelton had arrived in Malaya to assess the overall situation following the death of Sir Henry Gurney and the return home of Sir Harold Briggs on health grounds. His aim was to continue Briggs' work, instilling better communication between the military and the civil powers, but he wanted to place overall command of the colony in the hands of one man, responsible for all administration, both civil and military. Upon his return to Britain, he announced that General Sir Gerald Templer had been appointed High Commissioner of Malaya, effective from 7 February 1952.

Templer's aim was simple: to win, as he put it, the 'hearts and minds' of the Malayan population. He sought to instil faith in its people that the Federation was fighting for them, while at the same time paving the way for eventual independence, which it had already been conceded in London would come before the decade ended.

Early in 1952, an example of inter-services co-operation occurred when on 6 February a patrol of the Support Company commanded by Major Bob 'Beever' Martin was involved in a joint police and RAF Regiment operation at Serdang, west of Kajang.

Information received from an informer led the police to establish that a high-up member of the Malayan Communist Party who had a price of $8,000 on his head was hiding out in the jungle in a guarded camp. The man was known to have killed at least eight people in recent weeks, the last one brutally with a spade.

His camp was situated between a railway embankment and a road. It was decided that the RAF would man the embankment while the police manned the road. The battalion would then make a two-pronged attack. Major Martin's patrol would 'beat' from one end to the other, like a pheasant shoot, driving the bandits out into the fire of two further Suffolk patrols on the flanks. For the plan to work, all parties would have to hold their fire until they saw a target. The chance of friendly fire was high.

The operation began at first light with Major Martin's men shouting loudly at each other, deliberately alerting the bandits and forcing them to flee away from them.

Shortly afterwards, the first bandits were spotted in front and fire from a Bren gun was brought upon them.

Two bandits made for the railway embankment and were silhouetted on the rails. The RAF units, who had been recruited locally, brought fire upon them but failed to bring any of them down and instead drove them back into the path of Major Martin's men. The bandits then went to ground.

A bandit who was lying down in the undergrowth fired the first shot when he was almost trodden on by a member of the patrol. Armed with an old double-barrelled shotgun, he fired point blank at the approaching soldier, but the second barrel misfired. Another young Suffolk fired three rounds at him with his carbine.

Two more bandits who were hiding in the undergrowth then made a dash for it. Spotted by Lance Corporal 'Bos' Bostock of 3 Platoon, one was brought down by two rounds fired at him, but the other disappeared back into the jungle swamp and could not be found. Exhaustive searches for the next half hour could find no trace of him until the Iban tracker silently pointed to a tube coming up from under a large log in the swamp. The bandit was hiding under the water, breathing through a length of bamboo. A grenade was thrown in and his body was brought to the surface.

The action was described as 'a classic of its kind' and a reporter from *The Times* who was present wrote an article which concluded by noting that 'It showed how efficient British line regiments can be when they are all well trained and led.'[4] However, for that success, Private Humphrey Walker had been mortally wounded and later died of his injuries. He had been a member of the newly-reformed Assault Pioneer Platoon, arriving in Malaya in 1951. He had completed his basic training with the Bedfordshire and Hertfordshire Regiment before being posted to 1 Suffolk.

Now with 'kills' on the up, the rivalry between platoons intensified. Lieutenant Colonel Morcombe further pushed the competitive spirit that had been started by his predecessor Lieutenant Colonel Wight, and soon each platoon had a nickname and a platoon sign to accompany it.

No. 3 Platoon became 'The Phantoms', so named for the many months with missed opportunities at making contact with the enemy. No. 4 Platoon were 'The Death's Heads', but in 1951 they changed their name to 'The Angels'. No. 5 Platoon were 'The Panthers' and No. 6 Platoon became 'The Kangaroos' named, it was said, in homage to the Australian heritage of the battalion commander.

Platoons had names that reflected their experiences and the varied successes of their actions. No. 7 Platoon were named 'The Gravediggers' on account of an early patrol. They buried three bandits they had killed, but on returning to base they were requested to return, dig them up and bring the bodies in for formal identification.

No. 10 Platoon called themselves 'The Ladykillers', not for their prowess with the fairer sex but because of their first three kills, two of which were female bandits. Their platoon sign showed four puppies driving a jeep running over a fifth puppy.

The Support Company opted for a safe bet, calling themselves 'The Saints' supposedly because they always helped to 'save the day'. Their platoon sign, not surprisingly, carried the letter 'S' upon which sat a stickman with a halo, like Leslie Charteris' famous fictional detective Simon Templar, *aka* 'The Saint'. The mortar platoon had a touch of class – a winged mortar bomb falling, upon which the words 'Mortem Fugits' were written. Many proclaimed that it meant 'Death from Above'.

By 23 April 1952, the battalion's score stood at 135 bandits killed: 43 to 'C' Company, 44 to 'D' Company, 20 to 'A' Company and 18 to 'B' Company, while the Support Company had 7 and battalion HQ 3. An American reporter noted their competitive spirit and the continual drive for one-upmanship:

> Campaigning in Malaya has attractions for some young men. There is the patrolling and camping in the jungle, the building of temporary shelters, and cooking, coupled with the added excitement of fighting a war that is a very personal affair. Because they are stolid young men they show little awareness of the pain it can cause, except when one of their own is killed and then resentment only hardens the spirit. Because they are young and English they tend to see the war as a competition between companies and platoons. Outside C Company's office is a large notice reading '5 for 50'. This admixture of adolescent enthusiasm and ruthless professionalism obtains only in the jungle.[5]

On 26 April, the battalion finally got its first real 'break' into the Kajang Gang and its communication network. Piecing together information from an informer, a message discovered in a bandit pack the day before now confirmed that a meeting was being called for the following day in the area of Ulu Selangor with a number of high-up commanders of the Malayan Races Liberation Army.

Such was the importance of the information that it was agreed a patrol would be sent out immediately that night to lay an ambush for them. Rather than risk sending word out to companies to provide their best men, the Intelligence Officer Major Morgan stepped from the veranda of his office and picked the first five men from 'B' Company that he came across. Within minutes, he was off to the place mentioned.

Travelling from Kuala Kubu Bharu, Major 'Ernie' Morgan, along with Corporals Rolph and Laver and Privates Jay, Nightingale and Coe approached the rubber plantation in the early hours. They debussed and set off on foot with a police guide leading. Soon they were at the spot where the path climbed up from the plantation and Major Morgan set out his ambush position. By dawn, the men were placed on the high ground above and covered the track from all sides.

Four hours passed and the men waited in position with the mosquitoes taking their toll. Then at 0900 exactly as per the intelligence, figures came into view. First a woman, unarmed in traditional dress, and behind her four armed uniformed men. The party let the woman walk past the first two sentries before she spotted Corporal

Laver in the undergrowth. Before she could call out, the patrol opened fire on the main party. All fell, but the woman who ran on down the path stopped, threw a grenade back and ran on. It exploded harmlessly, but now the wounded bandits returned fire. They were swiftly silenced by the patrol.

Preparing to bring in the bodies for identification, the party set about finding suitable poles to which the corpses could be lashed for the journey back to base. Half an hour later, they were back at the debussing point where the truck was waiting for them. Within twenty minutes, they were back at the police station in Kuala Kubu Bharu where, after being photographed and fingerprinted, it was established that they had killed Long Pin and three of his close bodyguards.

This was a great milestone of achievement, both in the battalion and in the area as a whole. As commander of the 1st Regiment, Malayan Races Liberation Army and Selangor State Member of the Malayan Communist Party, Pin's death greatly weakened the bandit network in that area. It also confirmed that quick, decisive actions could bring about results, and that acting fast on information received from the police could pay dividends. The local press made much of his death:

> It was a textbook action. From information received, Captain Ernest Morgan and five men left at 3.00am in a jeep for a lonely side road on a rubber estate, and three hours later, at daybreak, were in position cunningly concealed on a slope where natural cover was sparse. For four hours they waited; then a woman, dressed as a rubber tapper, came into view, followed 75 yards behind by four uniformed terrorists. She came within inches of the patrol before she spotted them. All four terrorists were killed.[6]

After this successful coalition, the links between Special Branch and the battalion became much closer, with nightly intelligence briefings attended by the intelligence officer at the superintendent of police's bungalow. The High Commissioner General Sir Gerald Templer sent a signal to Lieutenant Colonel Morcombe congratulating them on their success and sent a photographer along to record the occasion. His signal was full of praise: 'Congratulations to all ranks concerned on your outstanding success this morning. Keep striking while the iron is hot. Well done!'[7] In the preceding twelve days, the battalion had killed eleven terrorists and recovered three rifles, a carbine, an old rusty Sten gun, three pistols and seven grenades.

A few weeks later came another success when a patrol by 2 Platoon, 'A' Company led by Second Lieutenant Pat Hopper was operating on the edge of the Kuala Langat swamp. For the previous three days they had been in the jungle before dawn, ready to ambush any parties on the likely routes. By the third day there was still no sign of the bandits, but just as they were about to turn back they came across a bandit camp.

Pots were on the fire cooking and packs were in the shelter. Suddenly four bandits were seen approaching and an ambush was sprung. Three were killed and one was wounded, who made off into the jungle. Despite a spirited chase by Second Lieutenant Hopper, the wounded man could not be found.

As was the custom, the bandits' bodies were brought back and displayed to the local inhabitants to prove that they were dead. While laying the corpses down on the ground, the locals started to mutter about one of them and he was soon identified as Loh Pin, the brother of Long Pin who had been killed by 'B' Company a few weeks before. It was later reported at home by the *News of the World* that Loh Pin had a price of £1,625 on his head, but sadly for Second Lieutenant Hopper, being a soldier he did not qualify to claim the bounty!

An American-Filipino reporter who accompanied his patrol wrote for the *Chicago Tribune*, praising the patrol in his article: 'I have seen armies in action in Korea, Indo-China and the Philippines, but these men in this platoon of the Suffolk Regiment were without a doubt the best in their field.'[8]

These actions prompted the local newspaper, the *Malay Straits Times*, to print a billboard that proclaimed 'Well Done Suffolks' and Second Lieutenant Richard Wilson was immediately dispatched into town to 'procure' a copy for the Regimental Museum. Despite these successes, however, the main prize still eluded them.

The leader of the Kajang Gang was the notorious Liew Kon Kim. A savage and brutal leader, he had in recent weeks become more active following the death of the Pin brothers. Kim was a tall and, unusually for a Chinaman, bearded terrorist.

He had a weakness for women and had several mistresses. He had been educated in a British school in Kajang and carried in his pocket an old compass, which he used to terrorize the local Chinese squatters by stating that it was a magical tool that would point to approaching enemy patrols. Having never seen a compass before, they lived in fear of him and his device.

Every time the battalion came close, Kim eluded them. Every time they thought they were on his trail, he managed to evade them. The most popular song sung in the battalion at that time was 'We haven't seen old Liew Kon Kim for a helluva time!' Then in late June 1952, their luck changed.

Information now came to the battalion that Kim was planning his next campaign against the security forces. On a routine roadblock, a member of 'C' Company found a loose handlebar grip on a rubber tapper's bicycle. Removing the grip, he found inside a small coil of paper with a message in Chinese written on it in tiny characters. After translation by Special Branch, it confirmed that Kim was still in the jungle and that he was now planning a raid on a tin mine near Broga.

The following day, another tapper dropped a wash bag when being searched and a policeman accidentally trod on a tube of toothpaste. Looking down at his feet, he saw that it contained a small file of paper. When cleaned, it gave further information that Kim was now in a camp deep in the jungle on the Kuala Langat Forest Reserve South.

Operation CHURCHMAN now swung into action to try to flush Kim out. On 29 June 1952, elements of 3 Platoon went out first to sweep an area to the north of where the bandits were believed to be and to try to push them southwards to where 'B' Company would be searching. Private Tony Coote remembered that first stage of the operation:

> Operation CHURCHMAN was one of the patrols that comes to mind, mainly because of the fact that my feet were so sore, having walked all night along a log track. We began at 4.30pm on the 1st July, finally getting back to base at 5.30pm on the 3rd July. We had been involved in phase one of this operation which began in the swamps but the bandits had already flown the area by the time we had got to their camp, but they left behind all the evidence of them having left there very recently.[9]

Early afternoon on 6 July 1952, a patrol of 5 Platoon, 'B' Company, led by Second Lieutenant Raymond Hands had just cleared the edge of the Kuala Langat Forest Reserve, south of Selangor on the edge of the New Brighton Estate. Here in the slushy overgrown swamp, the leading scouts, Private Baker armed with an Owen gun and Private Wyant armed with a Bren gun, spotted a lone bandit flitting across a log about 15 yards in front.

Immediately ditching packs, they headed off in pursuit. Followed by Second Lieutenant Hands, the three men came to a small clearing with what appeared to be a shelter built up on legs above the swamp. Seeing three people emerging at speed, Hands and the two scouts opened fire. The first was a man, who fell instantly to fire from Wyant's Bren, but the other two made off into the swamp. The second, a girl armed with a shotgun, fell after a burst from Hands' carbine, but the third, a man, was running off into the swamp beyond.

Following in pursuit and being guided by the splashing ahead of him, Hands opened up with a short burst. One bullet ricocheted from the pistol in the bandit's right hand, sending it flying into the swamp. Seeing the bandit falter but continue into the creepers, Hands followed cautiously for about 100 yards. A little further on he came across the body of the bandit, lying prostrate over a log. Still just alive, Hands emptied the remainder of his magazine into him.

No further movement ensued from the bandit and as Hands cautiously kicked the body over, worried the man could be concealing a live grenade, his face immediately revealed his identity. The full black beard proclaimed that it was none other than the 'Bearded Terror'. Immediately the rest of the patrol was behind him, staring in amazement at the body of Liew Kon Kim.

Though he spoke little of that day, Ray Hands later recalled the event:

> It was in the early afternoon. We walked into this clearing and there was a sleeping platform from which two people ran. I ran across the clearing and saw

the two people in front of me. Visibility if you remember being very limited – firing at noise rather than sight. The one was a girl, very young and armed with a shotgun, and the second was Liew Kon Kim himself. He was draped over a tree trunk, still alive as I recall. He must have had an awful lot of lead in him by then and it was a matter of a 'coup de grâce'.[10]

For the rest of the platoon it was a joyous moment. For more than two years the battalion had chased their almost mythical opponent around most of Kajang and Selangor with only a few fleeting contacts in between, but now they had finally got him. The patrol signaller, Private 'Sperry' Free, now made contact with Tac HQ: 'Two Baker to control. Have killed three bandits in a camp at UV. One has a beard and is thought to be Liew Kon Kim.'[11]

Upon hearing the message, 'B' Company's commander, Major Malcolm Dewar, immediately ran to his quarters and, after donning jungle greens and boots, rushed to the trucks to drive out to meet the returning patrol.

Back in the jungle, Hands was then preparing to bring in the bodies for positive identification, though there could be little doubt as to Kim's identity. He scoured the swamp and found Kim's pistol complete with a bullet mark on its grip and stuffed it in his pack. It was a Browning Hi-Power that had been dropped to the MPAJA at the tail end of the war. The following year he would donate it to the Regimental Museum. By the time the patrol had reached the road, the trucks were already there ready to take them back to camp, where a reception party was already gathering.

The local police were keen to capitalize on this hugely important milestone and straight away they informed the local press, who were flocking to the camp with photographers to meet the returning patrol. While Hands and his men posed for numerous photographs, Kim's body was being loaded into the back of a truck to be paraded through the outlying villages and settlements by the police to show the local inhabitants that the 'Bearded Terror' was now dead. The truck's driver Private Tony Rogers recalled their 'tour':

> After formal identification, his body was lifted onto the back of a very high GMC truck for the journey around the kampongs. Liew was still tied to a pole and I and another man who like me was rather short had difficulty in lifting him as his head was dangling. As we went forward his head struck the back of the GMC with a sickening 'thwack'. The colonel who was watching this was heard to remark 'Well, if he wasn't dead, he is now!'[12]

Within twelve hours, newspapers from Kuala Lumpur to Singapore bore front-page stories of the action, and within days the story had found its way home. The *Straits Times* masthead for 8 July 1952 was 'Beard Died After Tiffin – Three English youths found his hideout.' For a brief few hours, all Malaya shared in the battalion's success.

From their actions that day, the public and the wider world gained an understanding of the army's ongoing actions in Malaya, while at the same time it sent yet another message to the remaining bandits camped deep within the jungle that the security forces would not relent in their actions against them. No. 5 Platoon, in honour of their greatest achievement, promptly changed their name from 'The Panthers' to 'The Bearded Wonders' and a new platoon sign was quickly commissioned.

The bandits now knew from the papers exactly who had finally dispatched Liew Kon Kim and it was feared that a vengeance attack against Second Lieutenant Hands could be launched at any moment. With just a few weeks left to serve, his departure was brought forward, and after accompanying one final police patrol back to the location of the action, Hands was quietly posted home.

However, after that final patrol, Hands and a couple of his men were taking a well-earned swim when he was suddenly summoned. General Templer had arrived unannounced to congratulate him personally but there was no time for Ray to dress:

> I was presented to the General wearing a 'sarong' and to this day I have no idea what he said to me as my total concentration was focused on holding that piece of flimsy cotton up around my nether regions. No more embarrassing moment could be imagined than parading in front of your G.O.C. wearing a garment that required at least one and better two hands to preserve respectability. 5 Platoon must have looked seriously unmilitary that day![13]

Ray Hands, the shy, modest young man, was a National Service officer who had already made his intentions clear to the press: 'I am going up to Oxford and I am definitely not signing on for regular service.' For his actions that day he was awarded the Military Cross. Lieutenant Colonel Ian Wight noted later that the following were the skills possessed by junior officers such as Ray:

> One of the main strengths of the Battalion was that we had a remarkable number of outstanding junior leaders; the Starlings [Joe] the Kellys [Jimmy], the Dellers [Bill] and Hands [Ray] with remarkable powers of leadership and an ability not to get lost. Maintained by air supply, they were able to exist in the jungle for increasing periods and furthermore, the soldiers knew that they would never be abandoned by their comrades in the jungle and whatever the effort required they would be carried back to safety.[14]

Now more and more patrols were acting on the information of deserters who, having spent years in the jungle, were starting to see that their cause was lost and were now beginning to give themselves up.

When Second Lieutenant Pat Bird, a young National Service officer, arrived in mid-1952, he was posted to 'C' Company before being given command of 6 Platoon in

'B' Company. They were bottom of the leader board with just one kill in three months and Pat was determined to reverse their fortunes. He remembered his blunt introduction to the platoon by its Platoon Sergeant, Sergeant Smith: 'This platoon is the arse end of the battalion, Sir.'[15] However, within five months Pat had turned their fortunes around and increased their score to ten.

By August 1952, Surrendered Enemy Personnel (SEP) were giving themselves up at a rate of one man per week. Before the death of Liew Kon Kim, the average was two surrenders per month. The difficulties of using deserters could, however, present problems, as Pat recalled on one memorable patrol with his company commander, Major Malcolm Dewar:

> After about an hour's walk, following this chap, who did not appear to know the way that well, all sorts of things cross your mind – perhaps he was a double agent and leading us into an ambush? He certainly seemed scared almost witless at times, but he stood to make a thousand dollars or something if we killed anyone – a huge amount to him but he needed a certain amount of prodding with a loaded carbine to keep going.[16]

With the patrol in position, now came a real test of the deserter's information. Sometimes, after many hours of quiet waiting, nothing happened but on this occasion, Pat's patrol was lucky:

> A chap in khaki drill came towards our position down the track. You had to be very careful that he was alone, and not a scout for a larger group who would get away when you opened fire. He seemed to be alone. I don't think I was the first to open fire – I think it was Malcolm Dewar, or a chap who had a very good sighting. Anyway, everyone opened up after that and the chap lay dead on the track. We all gathered around and there was much jubilation, as this was the high point of four months of slogging through the jungle and having no contact with the enemy.[17]

Amid the celebration, the informer was kept closely guarded. The dead bandit was now examined:

> He was badly shot up, and had been shot through the head amongst other things, which had split open and his brains were hanging out and blood everywhere. No one would touch him – Malcolm Dewar turned away retching, Sergeant Smith, the old soldier, wouldn't go near him, so it was up to me to gather up his head in a plastic sheet and tie it all together. From that day on I began to acquire the grudging acceptance of Malcolm Dewar, who realised perhaps that not all National Service officers were effete intellectuals. It had to be done, and how could I ask anyone else to do it?[18]

For some, there was the morbid curiosity at seeing their first dead body. Often someone produced a camera and took a photograph of the dead bandit. Private George Flory of 1 Platoon, 'A' Company wrote home to his father telling him of their first 'kill' and enclosing a snapshot of the corpse:

> Well Dad, last week I went into action for the first time and we found a track, went up and came across a bandit camp. There were three bandits in it and we killed one and wounded one, so we got that for the Bt [battalion]. I have enclosed a snap of our kill but don't let Margaret [his younger sister] get hold of it. We killed him about 10 in the morning and we took him out onto the road where a lorry picked him up, then we went back on patrol. The next night with our officer we had a glorious drinking session; even the officer bought a round (21 pints!) and we all had bad heads next morning.[19]

Major Malcolm Dewar later praised the fighting efficiency of the National Serviceman: 'They're magnificent – and I know because my company is almost wholly National Servicemen.'[20] On an average patrol, only the officer or senior NCO would be regular soldiers, the remainder (more than 80 per cent) were all National Servicemen. The battalion commander, Lieutenant Colonel Philip Morcombe, also praised the efficiency and resilience of National Servicemen:

> It is a revelation to me to command a predominantly National Service battalion. They are so easy to teach. They have been terrific. Their endurance for lads of 18 and 19 is something I have never seen before. You can bash them like hell, give them a couple of hours' sleep, and they are fresh again.[21]

For his actions in Malaya Pat Bird was later Mentioned in Dispatches, the only National Service officer of the battalion to receive such an award during the campaign. Notification, however, arrived some twelve months later when the battalion was stationed in Trieste. This was because Malcolm Dewar 'missed the post' for submitting the form before they left Malaya!

August 1952 also saw the battalion reach its third year of operations. Traditionally, this was the end point of service where another battalion would be arriving to take over from them. However, at the pinnacle of their success, General Templer decided after personal consultation with Lieutenant Colonel Morcombe to extend their service for a further five months, giving him time in Selangor to complete his plans to eradicate the remainder of the Kajang Gang.

By 11 September 1952, the battalion had accounted for 173 bandits killed. 'C' Company now edged in front with 55, followed by 'D' Company with 50. 'A' Company had 29 and 'B' Company 27. The Support Company now had 9. Battalion HQ still only had 3, but all were now pushing to achieve a total of 200 before the tour expired.

The New Year of 1952 passed with a new sign being erected at Wardiburn Camp. Here Private Brinkhurst of HQ Company leans upon the sterling work of the Pioneer Platoon.

'B' Company office's notice board as captured in early 1952. Here 'Battalion Orders', along with the daily updated 'Part 1' and Part 2' orders, were displayed for information and it was a soldier's duty to read these each morning. Usually it was to his company office that a platoon commander or senior NCO was summoned to learn that he was 'out again' on patrol. Above the notice board was pinned a captured bandit flag – its hammer and sickle can just been seen under the thatch.

Happy and smiling, Private Sid Brace of 6 Platoon, 'B' Company gets ready to board a truck out on another patrol. Here Sid is armed with a No. 5 jungle carbine and carries a bandolier of additional ammunition tied around his waist. The shirt for the 1944 Pattern uniform and equipment can be seen being worn here with its distinctive shoulder patches to reduce the chafing of the pack when worn. Sid was originally called up for National Service with the Royal Norfolk Regiment, but was transferred to 1 Suffolk to be sent to Malaya. The remainder of his draft were posted to Korea.

Yet another patrol leaves with some happy (and some unhappy) faces. Despite the work that had to be done, the cheerfulness of these young men was undaunted. The Battalion's first commander, Lieutenant-Colonel Ian Wight noted that: 'The success which the Regiment achieved in Malaya depended in the main on the qualities in the Suffolk soldier. His ability to absorb soldiers from other Regiments and especially to imbue the many National Servicemen (conscripts) with his pride in his Regiment was the foundation from which success flowed.'

At times the jungle could be quite beautiful. Here, Second Lieutenant Richard Wilson captured an idyllic scene of a jungle stream overgrown with heavy foliage. The beauty of its interior, however, held numerous deadly hiding places for bandits.

Knee-deep in water, a patrol of 3 Platoon, 'A' Company trudges through the Kuala Langat North Swamp in early 1952. Weighed down with weaponry, the going was tough in such conditions. When patrols returned to base, foot inspections were held to ensure that the men did not develop any form of trench foot caused by spending prolonged periods in muddy water.

Exhausted under the weight of the Bren gun, Private Ron Newlands of 6 Platoon smiles for chum Sid Brace to take a picture. Behind him in the gloom, another member of the patrol smiles just as he is enveloped in the thick jungle foliage a few yards further down the path.

Boy of 19 who was left in charge wins DCM

A MALAYA jungle patrol, 12 men of the Suffolk Regiment, three days away from their base, were suddenly caught by heavy enemy fire.

The sergeant in charge and three other men were seriously wounded.

Acting L/Cpl. William John Price was left in command—20 yards from his nearest unwounded man and completely overlooked by the enemy, who outnumbered his force by three to one.

Hill captured

But he turned "what might have been a serious disaster into a considerable success," said the War Office last night, forced the enemy to break off the action, leaving three dead, secured a hill top, and established radio contact with base.

And so, on his next parade, 19-year-old National Serviceman William Price, of Glebeway, Hornchurch, Essex, will wear the Distinguished Conduct Medal.

L/Cpl Price
Three to one . . .

Lance Corporal William Price, who won the Distinguished Conduct Medal for his actions with 8 Platoon in 1951. Commanding a patrol of men when his sergeant and corporal had been wounded, he beat back a larger bandit force and safely evacuated his men. The *Daily Graphic* of 28 July 1951 told the story of the action that won Bill his award. His daughter later attended Regimental Functions, keen to meet with those who knew her father. In 2013 his medals were purchased with the assistance of the 'Friends of The Suffolk Regiment' and are now on display in the Regimental Museum.

A party at the Galloway Club in August 1951 to celebrate the battalion's 100th kill. Men of 'A', 'B' and 'C' companies in both 'civvies' and uniform celebrate this milestone of achievement. Suited in the foreground with drinks in hand are Major Alan Parkin and Captain Frank Lockett, both of whom it was said liked a drink. Note the hideously wide (and short) 'American ties'.

The Regimental Police have arrived to keep the peace, or maybe not so? It appears that an RP's armband and shirt have been 'procured' to put two defaulters under arrest. Note the police brassard with a cap badge in the centre with the letters 'R' and 'P'.

(**Above, left**) After a night of heavy celebration, the following morning patrolling continued as usual. Here Privates Jellaby and Ron 'Fuzzy' Knights of 9 Platoon, 'C' Company pause on patrol in the plantations. Note the No. 83 smoke grenades hung from Fuzzy's belt. He later signed on for regular service and served in the Corps of Drums.

(**Above, right**) Private Jellaby, or 'Jellyman' as he was nicknamed, crosses a precarious-looking log bridge upon exiting a squatters' settlement on the same patrol. They wear their packs slung loose over their shoulders, ready to ditch them quickly if need be.

(**Left**) Another Bren-gunner – this time Private Bob Duff of 5 Platoon – is seen on another patrol on the edge of Kuala Langat Forest Reserve in March 1952. Bob still lives in Ipswich and is believed to be one of the last survivors of 5 Platoon.

While a comrade rests on his poncho cape under their newly-erected 'basha', his chum gets on with supper. The sticks will support his mess tins over a small open fire. Water from his aluminium water bottle, the neck of which can be seen in the foreground, is ready in the other tin, while the contents of the cardboard ration box are opened and the biscuits are being unwrapped from their cellophane packet. Note the table cutlery being used as opposed to the seldom seen three-part interlocking knife, fork and spoon set that was issued with the 1944 Pattern equipment. In the background, almost unseen in the undergrowth, is another basha.

A brief stop and a quick drink from a coconut. This member of 6 Platoon can be seen with his Owen gun slung over his shoulder outside his basha. Curiously for use in the jungle, he has a pair of binoculars slung around his neck.

A long enough pause for a game of cards. Men of 5 Platoon stop and rest under an abandoned planter's bungalow where 'Sparky', the platoon's card sharp, plays a game with his fellow chums. His nickname can be seen painted on the brim of his jungle hat, which has the drawstring of a poncho cape threaded through its brim.

(**Above**) Second Lieutenant Pat Hopper stops for a smoke. Seated left with his M2 carbine, he is captured with his platoon sergeant, Sergeant Geoffrey Lister, and two men of 3 Platoon. Standing at the back on the left is Private Nick Paccito, who played football for the battalion and was also a crack shot. Pat would later rise to the rank of colonel and become a deputy lieutenant for Essex. The all important compass can be seen on a twisted lanyard around Pat's neck.

(**Opposite, above left**) 'With map and compass', Second Lieutenant Robin Farmer, 12 Platoon's commander, checks his patrol's position with the crucial compass while his batman Private Tredwell takes this snapshot of him. In a unique twist of fate, Robin's father had also commanded 12 Platoon of 1st Suffolk in Salonika during the Great War.

(**Opposite, above right**) Captain Alan Blackmore, an officer on detachment from the Royal Norfolk Regiment, is photographed on a logging trail in the Langat Forest Reserve. Though such tracks made getting into the centre of the swamp much easier, hours of trudging along them in flimsy rubber jungle boots could really hurt one's feet.

(**Below**) An artistic shot of Private Denis Lewin's Bren gun set up on its bipod in the jungle. In addition to his gun, his jungle hat and a primed No. 36 rifle grenade sitting on its baseplate can also be seen.

(**Above**) A demanding patrol and the men's exhaustion is clear from their faces as members of 5 Platoon, 'B' Company try to smile for the camera. Private Bernie Elmer, standing left, looks exhausted, as does Private Gough standing right. In centre at the back Private Wyant seems cheerful, as does Private Horribe in front. Long and arduous patrolling pushed men to the limits of physical endurance in the extremes of the climate.

(**Opposite, above**) A patrol of 1 Platoon, 'A' Company reaches a planter's bungalow and rests up before moving on. The stylized yellow 'castle' patches on their jungle hats can be clearly seen. Standing third from right is Private Dick May who was a huge supporter of the Old Comrades Association in his retirement, even giving over his back garden in Ipswich to hold fund-raising events for the Ipswich Branch.

(**Opposite, below**) The Battalion's in-house magazine the *Castle & Key* published in Malaya on a copying machine at Battalion HQ. It was an important tool in keeping up morale and also gave the men a chance to publish their views, uncensored by higher authority (though its contents were always checked by the Intelligence Officer before it was printed!) The *Suffolk Regimental Gazette* was the official organ of the Regiment. Published bi-monthly and then quarterly at home, its news contained reports from the Battalion, along with their comrades in the Territorial Army and the Old Comrades Association. Tracing its roots back to 1863, it was published almost continuously from 1890 until 1959.

THE CASTLE AND KEY

No. 15

31st March 1951

MONTIS INSIGNIA CALPE

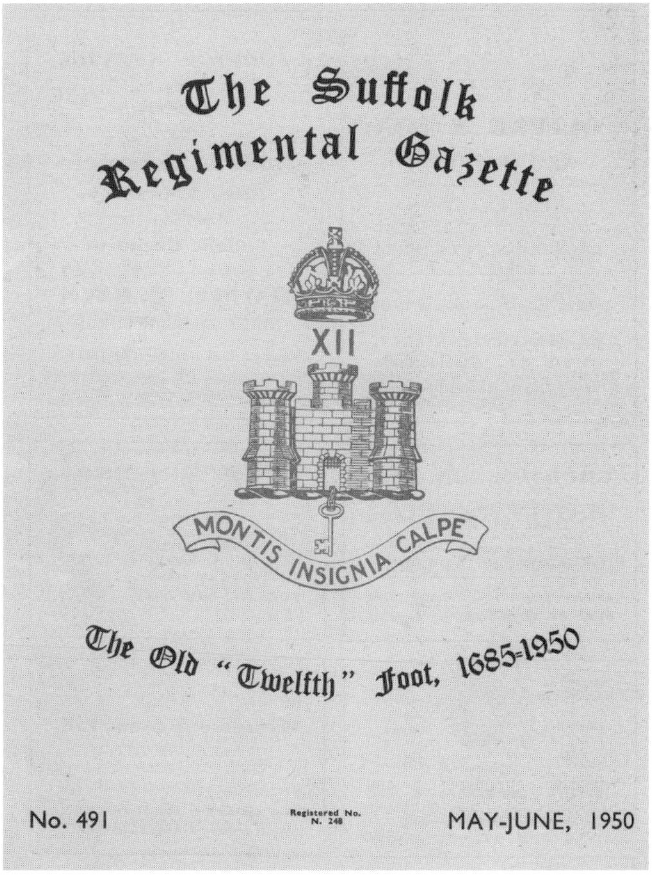

The Suffolk Regimental Gazette

XII

MONTIS INSIGNIA CALPE

The Old "Twelfth" Foot, 1685-1950

No. 491   Registered No. N. 248   MAY-JUNE, 1950

The platoon sign of 1 Platoon, 'The Hell Razors', featured a bat armed with a cutthroat razor in flight.

Lance Corporal 'Boz' Bostock stands beside the platoon sign of 3 Platoon, 'The Phantoms'. When this photograph was taken in early 1951, they had twelve 'kills' to their credit.

No. 4 Platoon was known originally as 'The Death's Heads' and had an appropriate platoon sign of a skull and crossbones. However, they changed their name in November 1951 to become 'The Angels'. This sign was the only one known to survive from Malaya. It was later hung on their barrack room door when the battalion was stationed in Trieste.

No. 5 Platoon was known originally as 'The Panthers', but after their successful elimination of the bearded bandit leader Liew Kon Kim they rechristened themselves as 'The Bearded Wonders'.

Private John Blench stands beside 6 Platoon's sign at Kajang. The platoon was known as 'The Kangaroos' in homage to the Australian heritage of the battalion commander, Lieutenant Colonel Philip Morcombe. In later life, John became a self-made millionaire, inventing a ploughing harrow that sold all around the world. He gave a free barbeque each year for his fellow Suffolk Regiment Malaya veterans on his farm near Peterborough until he died in 2012.

Possibly the largest platoon sign was that of 8 Platoon, 'The Green Devils', which it is believed was painted on the back of a trestle table. It featured the devil with a trident on the end of which was a bandit. In the background hanging over the tent frame are freshly-blancoed webbing gaiters and belts, no doubt in preparation for another parade.

THE
KANGAROO'S

6 PLATOON

8·PLN· "C" COY·

THE
GREEN
DEVILS

(**Above**) No. 9 Platoon was known as 'The Nutters'. They originally had a small sign that featured a 'nut' (in evening dress and bow tie) leaping over a crouching bandit, but by mid-1952 it had become old and worn. The 'Chief Nutter', Lieutenant Alan Horrex, was responsible for getting this replacement sign commissioned.

(**Opposite, above**) Dalmatians in a jeep riding over another dog was the sign of 10 Platoon, 'The Ladykillers'. They took that name because of the first 'kills' they scored in September 1949, two of which were females. Here Private John Hopkins poses beside it at Sungei Besi.

(**Opposite, below**) The Mortar Platoon's sign with the Suffolk Castle and Key in between falling mortar bombs.

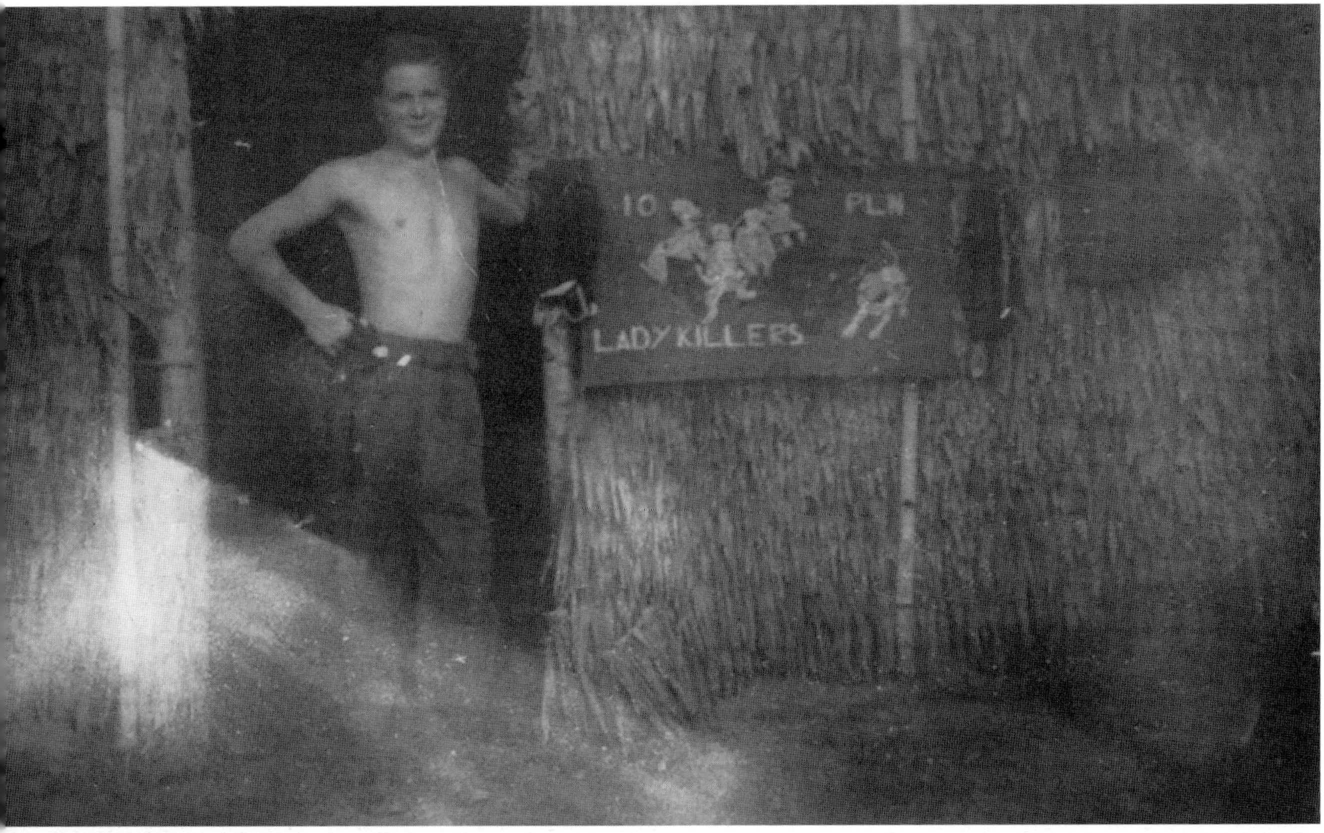
10
LADY KILLERS

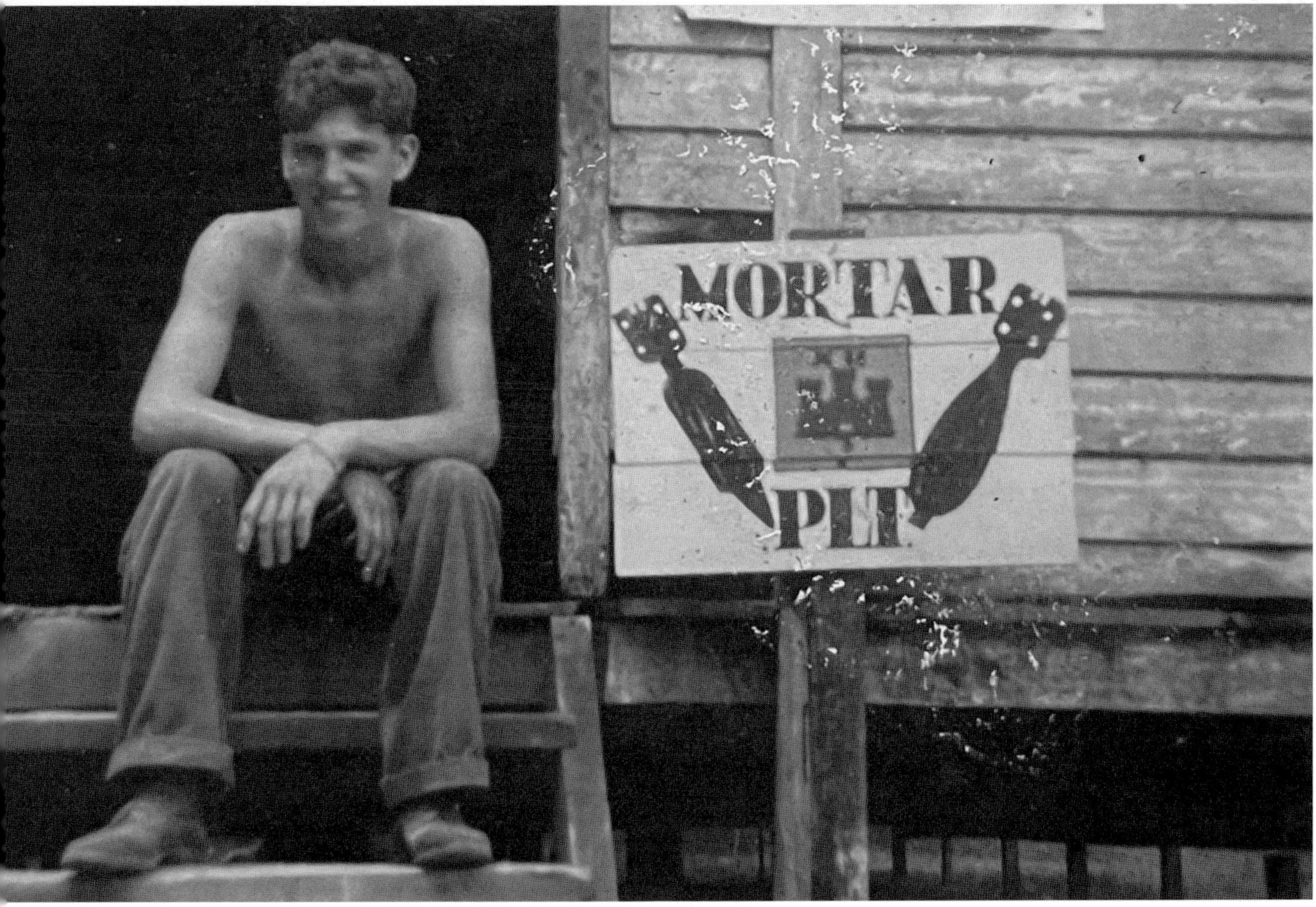
MORTAR
PLT

(**Opposite, above**) The MT Detachment's sign that hung outside the garages at Kajang. It featured the devil driving a jeep with a bellowing steam whistle. Sitting in the back, the Grim Reaper with his scythe looked out beyond.

(**Opposite, below**) The Signal Platoon sign photographed at Wardieburn in 1950. The crossed signal flags would have been familiar to many an old soldier in India before the war when they were the mainstay of communication between hill piquets. With the invention of wireless, their use in battle was greatly reduced.

(**Above**) Hustled out on patrol, Private Paul Coe of 4 Platoon awaits the transport to collect him before the deluge of tropical rain comes to engulf him. He is armed with an EY rifle and carries an additional cloth bandolier of fifty rounds of .303 ammunition tied around his waist.

The Long Pin ambush party, here captured with the patrol commander Major 'Ernie' Morgan, right. From left to right they are Privates Coe and Nightingale, Corporal Rolph, Private Jay and Corporal Laver. Major Morgan wears a black mourning armband for the recent passing of His Majesty, King George VI.

THE MEN WHO KILLED A $20,000 BANDIT—and it was a whisper that helped

THE PICKED TEAM of B Company Suffolk Regiment, who killed notorious Selangor bandit leader Long Pin on Saturday morning. Long Pin had a $20,000 reward on his head.

The Straits Times of Sunday, 25 May 1952, bearing the news that Loh Pin had been killed. To see one's regiment on the front cover was a proud thing and when copies soon disappeared from the local shops, someone had the bright idea of photographing a copy for those who did not possess one. This photo appeared in many Suffolk soldiers' albums.

'Suffolks Do It Again' was the billboard for *The Straits Times* of Sunday, 25 May 1952, and it was a much sought-after souvenir. A member of the battalion marvels at their accolade from the local press, while a member of the Federation of Malaya Police looks on. This photograph is believed to have been taken in the capital city, Kuala Lumpur.

Back at Wardieburn Camp, Private Smith of 4 Platoon holds a copy of the billboard for Lieutenant Richard Wilson to photograph it. This copy was later framed and presented to the Regimental Museum.

In June 1952, information came in that the bandit leader Liew Kon Kim was about to launch fresh attacks against the security forces in the area of the Kuala Langat swamps. 'A' and 'B' companies were sent there to commence Operation CHURCHMAN to try to locate him. The swamp comprised miles of 'lopak', a swampy, marshy shrub that when combined with tall, sharp grass such as that seen here made the going tough. Inside the swamp were small islands of higher, dryer ground where patrols could rest for the night and where the bandits usually made their camps.

On the afternoon of 6 July 1952, a patrol led by Second Lieutenant L.R. Hands found three bandits exiting a basha in the Kuala Langat South Swamp. His leading scout killed one and Second Lieutenant Hands accounted for the other two, one of which was identified as Liew Kon Kim, who had led a campaign of terror against civilians and the security forces alike for more than three years. For his actions that day Second Lieutenant Ray Hands was awarded the Military Cross.

Second Lieutenant Ray Hands with his two leading scouts — Private Wyant, left, and Private Baker, right — photographed outside battalion headquarters at Tanjong when the patrol returned to base with Kim's body.

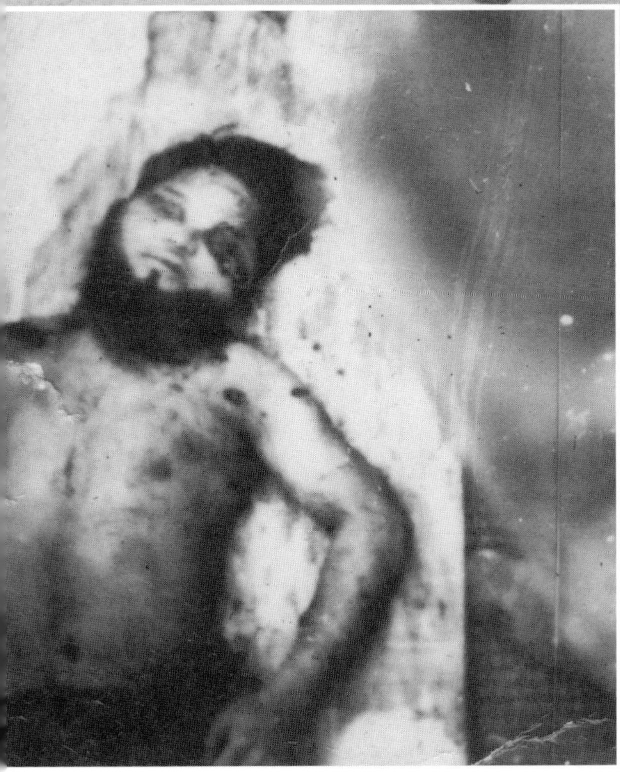

The entire patrol photographed after the event including the company commander. Standing left to right: Lance Corporal Atkins, Privates Duff, Hurlock and Gough, Sergeant Rinder, Private Baker, Lance Corporal Baggott, Major Dewar, Second Lieutenant Hands, Privates Grimwade and Baker, Lance Corporal Webster. Sitting left to right: Privates Jackson, Wiggins, Chapman, Blick and Horribe.

The bullet-riddled body of Liew Kon Kim photographed on the police station floor after it had been paraded around the local settlements and kampongs. Kim had waged war in Selangor since 1949 and many of his comrades had already been killed or captured by the battalion. Pre-dating Che Guevara's revolutionary pose by almost ten years, it was Lieu Kon Kim who first gave the world the image of the bearded rebel leader.

The Straits Times

MALAYA'S NATIONAL NEWSPAPER: ESTABLISHED 1845

TWELVE PAGES — SINGAPORE, MONDAY, JULY 7, 1952.

END OF THE BEARDED TERROR
Kajang Gang leader is killed with his mistress

KUALA LUMPUR, Sunday.

THE Federation's most notorious terrorist, Kajang Gang boss Liew Kon Kim—the bearded killer—was shot dead this afternoon by a young National Service officer of the First Battalion, the Suffolk Regiment.

With Liew died his mistress and one of his platoon commanders.

The shot which killed the bearded bandit probably saved the lives of seven people in a Selangor village.

For Liew Kon Kim had on him a list of seven names of people he had sworn to "liquidate."

JUBILATION IN TOWN

There was jubilation in Kajang, 15 miles south of Kuala Lumpur this evening when the news swept round the town.

But it could not match the jubilation in the camp of B Company of the First Suffolks, for today ended a personal battle which has gone on for three years, almost to the day, between the Suffolks and the bearded terror.

It was also the B Company who killed Long Pin, the regimental commander of Selangor's terrorists, in April.

Liew Kon Kim, alias Chow Wah, alias Voo Soo, was commander of No. 4 Independent Company of No. 1 Terrorist Regiment.

Last Wednesday, the First Suffolks, supported by the Special Air Services Regiment, the Royal West Kents, the Royal Artillery, police and home guards, launched "Operation Churchman" with the declared intention of "getting" Liew Kon Kim.

The troops moved into the north end of Kuala Langat south forest reserve, which is south of Brooklands Estate in south-west Selangor. With a regular flow of information from the police special branch in Klang, they made five con-

★ See Page Five

DAILY MIRROR

He leaves school—wins MC

Studious Ray kills bearded terror chief

SECOND Lieutenant Leslie Raymond Hands, the studious boy who went straight from school to the Army, was last night awarded the Military Cross.

The award was for killing Liew Kon Kim, the "bearded terror," one of Malaya's most feared bandit leaders.

Lieutenant Hands, 20, is an undergraduate now of Lincoln College, Oxford. He was demobilised this year after completing his National Service.

Price on His Head

He was leading a platoon of the Suffolk Regiment in South Selangor last July, with orders to kill Liew Kon Kim, the man with a price of £3,500 on his head.

During the patrol, without any warning, an armed terrorist ran across a swamp. Lieutenant Hands, not long before a schoolboy at Hurstpierpoint College, fired and chased him. The man ran to a shelter. Then from it three armed bandits came out.

Lieutenant Hands shot the first. The others ran into the swamp. He chased them and in fifty yards shot a second one. The third bandit went crashing through the swamp. Lieutenant Hands caught him in 100 yards—and shot him.

Then Lieutenant Hands recognised him as Liew Kon Kim, the terror of the district for three years.

The official citation says: "This officer has demonstrated the highest example of dash and personal bravery under the most adverse and difficult physical conditions."

'Just Likes Books'

Last night, at their house in Vernon-avenue, Woodford Green, Essex, Raymond Hands's parents said: "We are very proud of him." His father went on: "We never thought of him as an outstanding soldier boy.

"He was in his school Cadet corps, but he just likes books, that's all. The three years at Oxford are just what he has longed for."

The award to Lieutenant Hands was announced in the "London Gazette." The award of a knighthood to Major-General A. J. H. Cassels, D.S.O., former commander of the 1st Commonwealth Division in Korea, was also announced.

The killing of the notorious bearded terrorist, Liew Kon Kim captured front pages across the east. Here *The Straits Times* ran the story two days running showing a smiling Second Lieutenant Ray Hands being congratulated by his Battalion Commander, Lieutenant Philip Morcombe. The *Daily Mirror* at home recorded the event and made much of the story of Ray Hands being the shy bookworm turned bandit hunter.

The Straits Times

MALAYA'S NATIONAL NEWSPAPER: ESTABLISHED 1845

TWELVE PAGES SINGAPORE, TUESDAY, JULY 8, 1952.

'BEARD' DIED AFTER TIFFIN

Three English youths found his hideout

He fired the shot...

SECOND LIEUT. RAYMOND HANDS, the man who fired the shot which killed Liew Kon Kim, is congratulated by his O.C.

THE FACE OF A SHY HERO ...... Bashful Second Lieut. Hands......

Oxford for me, says hero

SECOND Lieutenant Hands, a shy young man, next month finishes his two years in the Army and is due to leave for England. He said: "I am going to Oxford—and I am definitely not signing on for regular Army service."

'SUCH SURPRISE'

KUALA LUMPUR, Monday.

THOUSANDS of new villagers in South Selangor today gaped at the bullet-riddled body of the man who for four years had terrorised them. Emergency Information Services loudspeaker vans toured the area announcing: "Liew Kon Kim is dead."

The killing of Liew yesterday afternoon has been a great boost to morale in South Selangor—and a very serious blow to the terrorists.

He used to boast: "I'll never be killed." He took good care to give the Security Forces as little chance as possible. He kept out of the way in the jungle as the battles went on.

Yesterday afternoon he thought he was far enough away from danger. His men were in the north of the Kuala Langat south forest reserve.

THE RADIO WAS ON

So were the 1st Suffolk Regiment, the Special Air Service Regiment, and the Royal West Kents. In the north was where the Royal Artillery were dropping their shells and the R.A.F. their bombs.

Liew was in a small but comfortable hideout in the south of the forest reserve. With his mistress Ah Yin, his vice-commander, Kong Fah, and two of his men, Liew was sprawled out on the floor of his jungle hut, listening to a radio and drinking coffee after a good tiffin.

Then at 2.30 the end came for Liew—and for his mistress and his vice-commander.

Three young Englishmen, all under 20, walked into the camp.

Second Lieutenant Raymond Hands, Private K Baker and Private W. Wyant, of "B" Company, 1st Battalion, Suffolk Regiment, all National Servicemen, had been scouting ahead of their platoon when they found themselves in the middle of Liew's camp.

'Bit of a shock'

Lieutenant Hands said today: "My platoon was the centre of three platoons in the jungle north of Tumsoh Malay reserve.

"We were of cour...

...and he died

...AND THE BEARDED TERROR HE KILLED. Liew Kon Kim, seen in this picture with one of his mistresses, Loh Yuk Mooi. She was killed by security forces last year.

"BEARDED WONDER" DIES IN FOREST

Had List Of Seven He Wished To Eliminate

INFORMATION BETRAYS "ASTUTE AND DARING COMMANDER"

(Malay Mail Reporter)

The "bearded wonder," who had terrorised the Ulu Langat district since the emergency began, and was responsible for most of the atrocities in that area, met his fate yesterday at the hands of the Suffolks Regiment. He was an old enemy of the irs.

The man was 32-year-old Liew Kon Kim, the bearded leader, who had a price of $13,000 on his head and was the leader of the terrorist forces in South Selangor. He was shot dead by 2/Lieutenant Raymond Hands of No. 5 platoon of the Suffolks Regiment in South Selangor.

Liew Kon Kim was killed with Kong Fah, a platoon commander, and his own mistress, Ah Ying.

The contact took place in the course of an operation planned to destroy the "bearded wonder," who was known as an astute and daring commander.

The operation was mounted on the morning of July 2 and a force of the Suffolks, with detachments of the Malayan Scouts, the Royal West Kents, Royal Artillery, Police and Home Guards took part. An extensive search was made in the Kuala Langat forest.

...AND THE BEARDED TERROR HE KILLED. Liew Kon Kim, seen in this picture with one of his mistresses, Loh Yuk Mooi. She was killed by security forces last year.

Another clipping of the Liew Kon Kim story. Photographs of the 'Bearded Terror' were few and far between. The image seen here and in other articles was over a year old and had been found in a captured bandit pack by a member of the Battalion.

Such was the speed of the attack, that complete surprise was affected on Liew and his comrades. As this article noted, their freshly brewed coffee was still hot when their camp was attacked.

Bearded Liew left his coffee

★ From Page One

a big black beard and with a Browning 9mm pistol in his hand. We were sure he was Liew Kon Kim. The woman was wearing black trousers and a blouse and had a shot gun in her hand.

"In the hut the radio—a portable battery set—was still playing.

"The gang had been drinking coffee when we got them and the coffee was in the cups and still hot. It was a pity to waste it so we drank it. It was sweet and there was no milk, but we were glad of it after going through swamp up to our necks.

"It was a nice camp and they seemed to be doing themselves well. We found fresh tomatoes, lettuce and vegetables and a good amount of other food.

'But they obviously did not expect visitors because the wireless was blaring and they had no sentries out."

The soldiers got the three bodies out of the jungle with great difficulty and it was dark when they arrived back at their base in Batu Laut village

The tired men of "B" Company 1st Suffolks, "had a terrific celebration" last night.

One officer said today: "For three years our battalion has tried to get Liew Kon Kim. We have laid on dozens of traps and big operations but he always got away"

But the whole operation, which started last Wednesday, was planned with the object of getting Liew Kon Kim.

Major Malcolm Dewar, commanding officer of B Company, 1st Suffolks, said: "We are very proud of our success.

"Though our company has the lowest number of kills in the battalion our motto is quality and not quantity. We have bagged all the big boys on the Suffolk scoreboard —Maniam, the Tamil Communist boss in North Selangor, Long Pin, the regimental commander for Selangor, and now Liew Kon Kim and his vice-commander."

So notorious was Liew, the bearded killer, that in 1949, before a general scheme of rewards was introduced, the police put a price of $30,000 on his head—making him as important as any of the Federation's leading Communists.

Though only a company commander and worth $13,000 alive in the present scale of rewards, Liew's actual value is estimated to be as high as $100,000.

The Suffolk Regiment is now receiving a stream of congratulatory telegrams The first to arrive was from the former OSPC of Kajang, Mr. Peter Andrew, who had a great deal to do with planning operations against Liew with the Suffolk Regiment.

General Sir Gerald Templer congratulating all ranks "who were in at the kill of the notorious Liew Kon Kim" said all law-abiding citizens in the Kajang area would be encouraged by their exploit.

From the Mentri Besar, Selangor, Raja Uda, on behalf of the State War Executive Committee, came a telegram saying: "Splendid work. Thanks for ridding South Selangor of Public Enemy Number One."

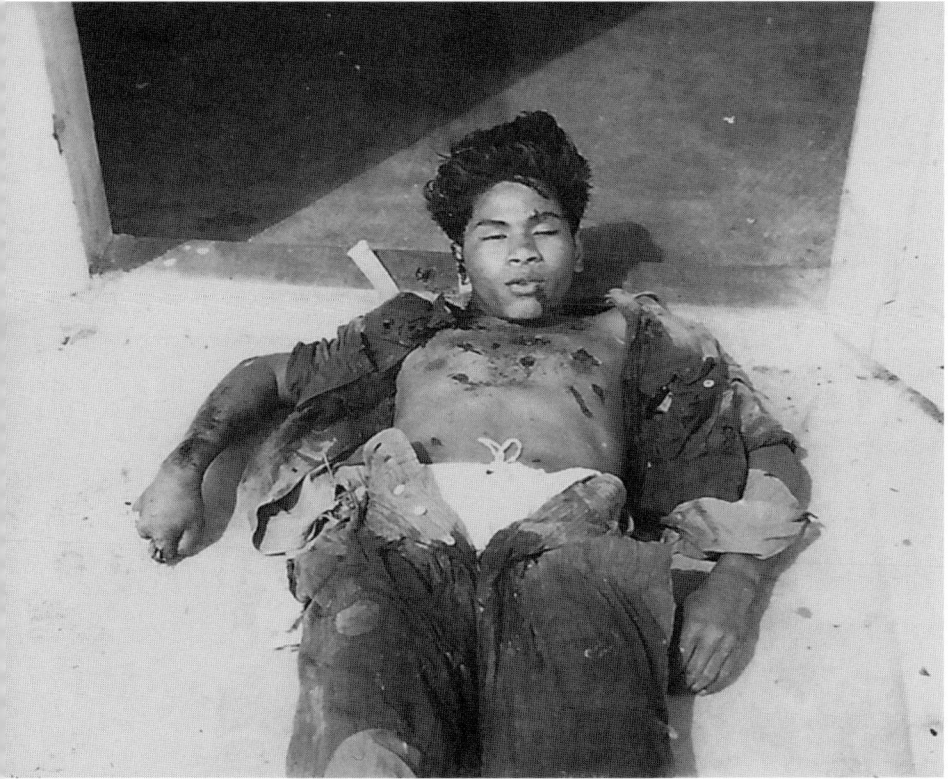

Other bandits killed by patrols in the Kuala Langat swamps are photographed at Tanjong.

(**Opposite, above**) On the other side of the press cameras, the battalion commander Lieutenant Colonel Philip Morcombe talks with the local chief inspector of police while local tribal and community leaders arrived to view the body of Liew Kon Kim. The police saw to it that by morning news of Kim's death was in as many newspapers in Malaya as possible.

(**Opposite, below**) With the euphoria over, it was back to patrolling again. Under the watchful eye of the platoon sergeant, Lieutenant Alan Horrex and a tracker discuss the route out for the next 9 Platoon patrol. The sergeant carries a No. 36 grenade tucked onto his belt on his right hip and held in place by a loop that was designed to hold the rifle butt when on the march.

(**Above**) Preparations for a patrol by 4 Platoon. Here at Sungei Besi, Private Fred Mullinder, right, helps in the distribution of rations. The straight-sided tins contained everything from stewed steak to fruit salad, with oatmeal blocks and biscuits in lieu of bread. Sergeant Fowler, standing left with his trademark pipe, gives out the small portable stoves used for heating food and boiling water. These stoves, which had three fold-out legs, were fuelled by a round hexamine tablet that burned ferociously when lit. They were contained in a small tin sealed with cotton tape.

(**Above**) A patrol of 5 Platoon is briefed by their platoon sergeant before boarding trucks to take them to their jungle entry point. Some members of the patrol carry their small packs with their poncho capes rolled underneath. The soldier standing second left with his back to the camera carries a shell dressing bag with the patrol's limited first-aid equipment. The patrol commander also carried a small first-aid pouch known as a 'J Pack', which contained morphine syringes as well as various ointments and dressings.

(**Opposite, above**) Up in the Batu hills, Second Lieutenant Robin Farmer is captured by Corporal Jimmy Kelly's camera. After completing his National Service with the regiment in Trieste, Robin went up to Oxford and later joined Imperial Chemical Industries (ICI), travelling the world heading up new export divisions of the company. He later worked for the National Health Service in Cheshire.

(**Opposite, below**) Sometimes a patrol took the men out to the edges of the newly-created 'kampongs'. Inside, free from the intimidation of the bandits, its newly rehoused inhabitants benefited from clubs and amenities, schools and doctors. Here a kampong is viewed from outside the wire by a passing patrol of 9 Platoon.

Whenever the soldiers came into the camps, they attracted a crowd. Here Private John Hopkins of 10 Platoon makes contact with base on his patrol's No. 18 wireless set to the wonder and amazement of the local schoolchildren. It was with such simple acts that the battalion gained the trust of the locals; the crucial 'hearts and minds' policy advocated by General Templer.

Some hours into a patrol and exhaustion is beginning to take its toll. Private Sid Brace in the centre looks none too happy to pose for a fellow comrade's camera. Long patrolling wore down the men's spirit, but after sufficient rest they were ready to start all over again the next day. The battalion commander praised the resilience of National Servicemen and their ability to go on patrolling day after day.

(**Opposite, above**) Back at their base in the rubber factory, this day patrol of 11 Platoon, 'D' Company is paraded for a weapons inspection. Magazines have been removed from weapons and are held ready for inspection. The Brengunner, third right, appears a little slow on the uptake for his Bren still has its magazine in place.

(**Above**) When platoons were deep in the jungle on long-range patrols, they frequently went outside the range of their radio set. Here a radio truck of the battalion is parked at the jungle's edge to act as a relay station from the patrol to battalion HQ.

(**Opposite, below**) Private John Hopkins poses on top of a Humber scout car, mounted with twin Vickers 'K' guns. All the battalion's vehicles were named after regimental battle honours and here 'Gibralter' signified the regiment's participation in the Great Siege of 1779–83, although one hopes that the spelling was eventually corrected!

(**Above**) A pair of twin Brens that were mounted on top of a Humber scout car. The wire flex was to a spotlight that was fixed to the trajectory of the guns and helped at night to locate their fire. The steel levers positioned through the triggers were used to control their fire from within the car; much safer than the old method of pulling a lanyard.

(**Opposite, above**) The regimental contractor Khan M.A. Hamid had a party of 'char wallahs' that followed the battalion out to the jungle with their urns of tea, and were usually ready for them when they returned. Here they have accompanied this platoon out to the ranges for the day.

(**Opposite, below**) Back on the range again, this time practising with the hugely disliked flame-thrower. It was a dangerous and much mistrusted weapon among those who had the 'privilege' of using it.

As new drafts of National Servicemen continually arrived to serve with the battalion, all of them spent time on the ranges to be introduced to the various new weapons they were to use. Here in newly-issued webbing and jungle greens, men practise with the older Mk 5 Sten gun and the Owen submachine gun. Both weapons were chambered in 9mm.

The EY rifle with its cup discharger was capable of firing a rifle grenade like a mortar. Such was the velocity of the charge required to get it airborne that it had to be fired from the ground like a mortar. However, the more daring man could, in the heat of the moment, fire it from the shoulder as seen here.

Private Denis Lewin poses with an Owen gun at Kajang in 1952. A good view can be seen of the long webbing sheath for the machete. The 1944 Pattern equipment was designed down to the last detail, taking care to consider all the soldiers' needs and wants along with their comfort, but it was the machete that always seemed to get in the way, banging continuously against the carrier's leg as he stomped through his patrolling.

In December 1951, the Secretary of State for the Colonies, the Rt Hon Oliver Lyttelton, later Lord Chandos, visited the battalion on a tour of Malaya. Here he inspects a patrol under the command of Lieutenant Mike Benn, second right, accompanied by Major Tim O'Reilley, left. Known as 'Ticker' Benn on account of his height (as in 'Big Ben'), he served with the battalion for more than a year on transfer from the Royal Army Ordnance Corps (RAOC). He is armed with an M2 carbine and carries the patrol's compass on a lanyard around his neck. Benn later served in Korea. His tracker 'Jawa' can be seen third left, with his hair down.

Sergeant 'Mick' Rinder, 5 Platoon's sergeant, photographed here at Wardieburn in early 1952 when just off on patrol. Armed with an M2 carbine, he appears to have a native knife or dagger pushed into his waist belt. In his hat is tucked the all-important tin opener. Rinder was awarded the British Empire Medal in 1953 for his actions in Malaya. His citation noted that 'he has proved himself completely reliable, and an NCO who can be entrusted to carry out the most difficult operation with success.'

(**Above**) Tapping into the local telephone system was a skill that could come in handy in most difficult situations, particularly when an urgent message could not get through via wireless. Here Corporal Lee takes down an urgent message relayed by Sergeant Tom Mansell, who is on the telephone.

(**Opposite, above**) Minden Day – the annual commemoration of the regiment's principal battle honour, held annually on 1 August – began in 1952 with an inspection by Brigadier W.H. Lambert commanding 18th Independent Infantry Brigade, who spoke impressively about the fine traditions of the regiment in 1759 and how then, 193 years later, they were still upholding them in Malaya.

(**Opposite, below**) After the brigadier's speech, the battalion led by Lieutenant Colonel Morcombe marched past in company order. Here Major Tim O'Reilley, then commanding 'A' Company, marches past, his sword dipped in salute. He is followed by Second Lieutenant John Crowe who then commanded 1 Platoon. To his left is Company Sergeant Major Colleen. All ranks wear roses in their headdress in honour of the regimental custom.

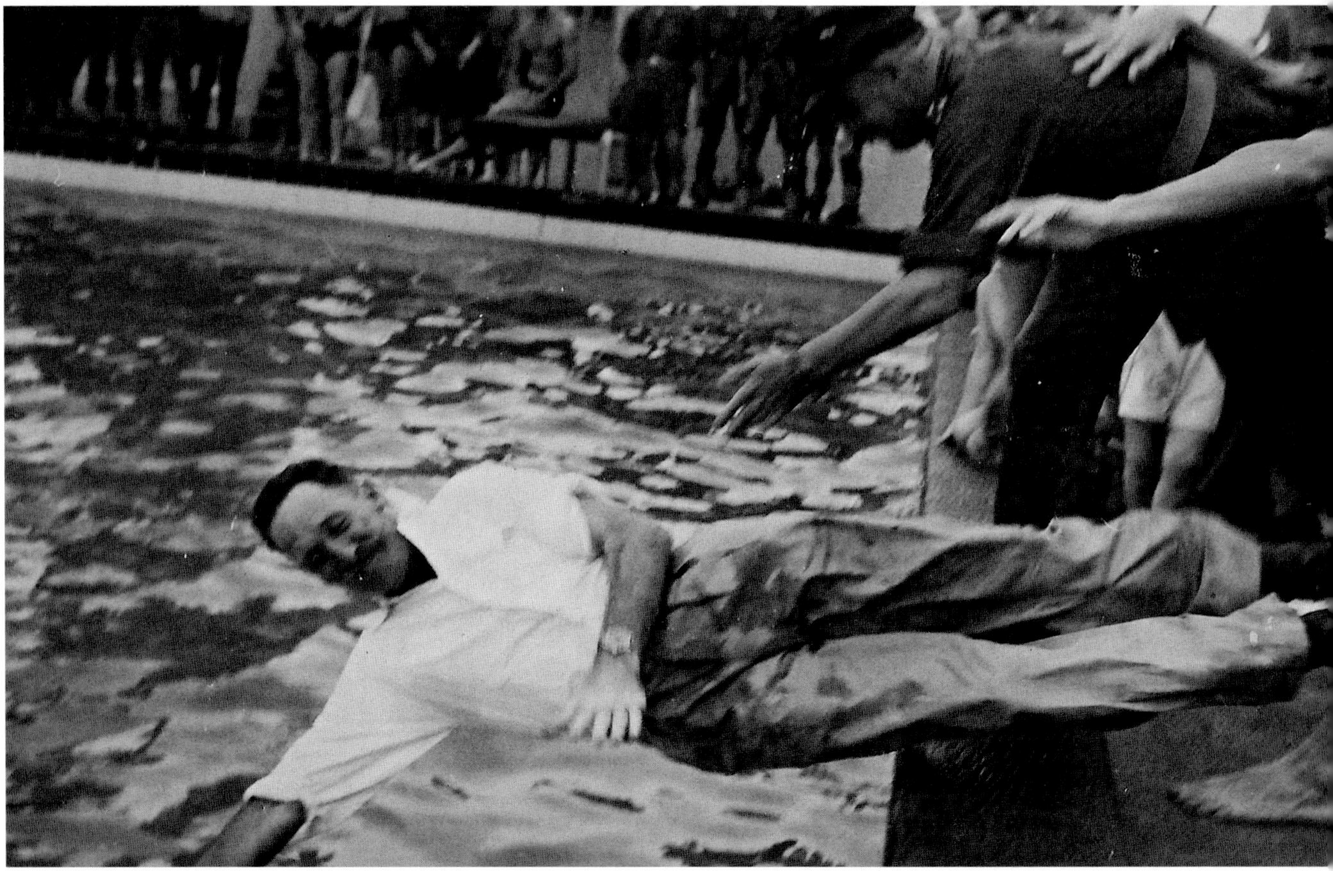

(**Opposite, above**) After the formal parade, in the afternoon an inter-company swimming gala was held. Now in civilian dress, Lieutenant Colonel and Mrs Morcombe and their son Simon arrive to watch the event. Mrs Morcombe wears a diamond and platinum brooch in the form of a regimental cap badge, but all still wear their roses including Captain Frank Lockett who is seen behind with roses pinned to his shirt.

(**Opposite, below**) As the festivities continued, so did the japes. Here the regimental sergeant major RSM Duffy is launched into the pool fully clothed, with more than a helping hand from the Intelligence Officer Major Morgan.

(**Above**) The festivities included a tombola and games for the children of the battalion. Here two corporals in sarongs and headscarves man the 'three darts to win' stall. On the table in front of them are the prizes: tins of cigarettes, a bottle of English beer, Chinese 'worry' dolls, a regimental china beer tankard and a tin of Yardley's talcum powder.

Chapter Five

The Race for 200

Towards the end of the battalion's service, news came that a film was to be commissioned about the Emergency. Events in Korea had overshadowed the still ongoing Emergency in Malaya and it was felt that the public at home should be better informed as to the importance of the role the British army was performing there in support of the civilian administration. As the 'top' battalion operating in Malaya, 1st Suffolk were to play a lead role in several re-enacted scenes that were to be created for the benefit of the camera.

Under director David MacDonald, 12 Platoon 'D' Company were detailed to re-enact an average two-day patrol that would culminate in the storming of an enemy camp. Speaking parts went to Major Eric Lummis as 'D' Company commander and to Second Lieutenant Robin Farmer commanding 12 Platoon. Sadly his platoon sergeant Harry Aldridge had a very broad Northamptonshire accent which wasn't quite gruff enough, and his voice was later dubbed into soft Cockney by John Slater, an actor known for playing such types in the films *A Canterbury Tale* and *Passport to Pimlico*.

The final product was titled *Operation Malaya* and was released in August 1953. Though not a sell-out at the box office, the film was the only semi-documentary film on the Malayan Emergency produced during the conflict.

In its final months in Malaya, the battalion received several visits from travelling performing troupes organized in the main by the Selangor Forces Amenities Fund. The actor Brian Reece, better known as 'PC 49' in the BBC radio series at home, toured British units in the Far East with the Donald Peers show and visited 'B' Company at Kajang. After a hilarious performance, the girls of the troupe posed with the men of 4 and 6 platoons and later shared a drink with them.

Another entertainer, Bert Brownbill, came to Kuala Kubu Bharu to entertain men of 'B' Company. Bringing with him several girls from his London show, he spent much time afterwards talking with the men. When he returned home in late 1952, he wrote to the relatives of many of those serving with the battalion including Private Bernie Elmer's mother, who then ran a pub in Great Yarmouth:

> I have just returned from Malaya with the Donald Peers' show, and whilst visiting Kajang I had the pleasure of not only entertaining the 1st Bn. of the Suffolks but

of meeting your boy also. I had quite a chat with him after the show and promised him I would drop you a line to give you this personal message which is 'Don't worry, everything's going to be alright.' He was looking extremely fit and despite incredible hardships and heat, he was very cheerful. As you have read in the papers, the Suffolk boys are great fighters and it was our privilege to be with them just before they got Liew Kon Kim whom they had been after for over two years. Going out fresh from England it was heartening to see the magnificent way in which these boys have adapted themselves to this vicious jungle warfare, and I was most impressed with the extremely high standard of morale, for those boys are doing a wonderful job and certainly maintaining the highest traditions of the British Army.[1]

On 22 November, a seven-man 'D' Company patrol which was led by Major Eric Lummis made contact with two bandits on the edge of a rubber plantation at Sungei Merbau. One bandit was dressed in civilian clothes, but the other bandit was dressed in khaki drill and was wearing a Special Constable's beret. In the seconds during which each party spotted one another, they waited for someone to make the first move.

The two bandits made off into the lalang and the patrol followed. The bandit in the beret waded into a small stream and upon reaching the opposite bank, turned and threw a grenade back. Spotted by Major Lummis who shouted 'Grenade!', it lay smoking as he jumped over it and ran on in pursuit. It had failed to explode and as the bandit then raised his rifle (a captured No. 5), quick as a flash a member of the patrol, Private John Myhill, aimed and shot him.

Immediately the remainder of the patrol opened up on the other man, who was seen to weave and stagger badly wounded between the trees but disappeared into the undergrowth. The dead bandit was identified as Tit Liew and the serial number of the rifle identified it as being one lost in a police ambush in June 1951.

Liew was known to be a cruel and sadistic leader who had in the previous days killed three Min Yuen at Sungei Chua. He was known to be an exceptionally heavy smoker and the heavy tobacco staining up to the knuckles on his hands soon confirmed his identity. In his pack were found pictures of Lenin and Stalin. His death brought the battalion's score to 186 plus a front-page newspaper article that ran 'Private Myhill was too quick for the Bandit Leader'.[2]

The final loss to the battalion came on 25 November 1952 when a patrol of 5 Platoon, 'B' Company under the command of Second Lieutenant Martin Knowles contacted a party of bandits in the Tanjong Duablas Reserve plantation. A patrol earlier that day under the command of Second Lieutenant Pat Bird had contacted two terrorists, killing one, and was in the process of making their way back with the body when they met Second Lieutenant Knowles' patrol going out.

At 1430 Martin's patrol made contact with bandits on the edge of the Kuala Langat swamp, as he later recalled in graphic detail:

> Suddenly one of my men turned and said he had seen two figures in KD cross in between positions. I grabbed the nearest section (an Owen-gunner, Bren-gunner, rifleman, Lance Corporal Mallows and 4 Platoon's Iban 'Ijoh'). Soon we found their tracks and the Iban took the lead, closely followed by Jackson, the Owen-gunner and myself. Nose to the ground, we snaked our way after them, flat out, puffing and panting.[3]

Now in the swamp, the boggy ground made the going tough and soon all were caked in mud. Then suddenly, fire was brought upon them:

> There was a loud bang and a bullet whistled past the Iban's ear. We flung ourselves to the ground and fired back as hard as we could; Private Hall, my Bren-gunner firing close between the heads of Jackson and the Iban. We heard the bandits break away through the tangled creepers and soon we came across a pack they had dropped off. One of them was a woman; we could smell her perfume. The Iban said that one was barefoot. We followed out of breath and struggling through the mud, creepers and other obstacles. Again we saw them and fired but still no results. When we had gone about 1,500 yards in all we crossed a large log. The Iban, Jackson and myself were over, the others coming across abreast when suddenly the bushes 15 yards ahead opened up and a Bren gun fired on us on automatic.[4]

With bullets flying, they lay flat to the ground. Then, when the fire died down, the reality struck that a member of the patrol had been hit:

> I heard a terrible groaning behind me and when the first burst was over Hagger called to me from behind the log and said that Lance Corporal Mallows had been hit badly. I called up Hall to give a burst with the Bren and then I crawled back to where Mallows lay while others came behind the log. He was lying as he had fallen. A burst had caught him in the left shoulder and his arm was nearly off. One bullet had gone just above the heart. I felt his pulse and laid my hand on his body. He was ghastly white and had stopped breathing. Jackson said 'Is he dead?' 'Yes, he's dead.' 'The poor bugger.' Hagger turned a white face towards me and said 'Let's get back. Let's go.'[5]

An examination by Corporal Cooper of the spot from which the bandit had fired revealed fifteen empty .303 cases, but the bandit had fled into the deep undergrowth with his Bren, most probably hidden since the war.

Firing three shots with a Very pistol for assistance, the patrol now gathered branches to construct a makeshift stretcher. Mallows' poncho cape was then tied between them and braced with rifle slings. Moving back along the way they had come, after some time they met a section of 1 Platoon under Second Lieutenant John Crowe who had followed them when he had seen the flares. As evening came the two patrols trudged on together, finally leaving the muddy swamp behind them:

> John went ahead but could not get through the belukar [scrub or bush], so he returned and we lay down in the water and tried to sleep. We had no food and the last meal had been at 5.15 that morning. Cigarettes ran out and it rained between two and four o'clock in the morning. It was cold and the mosquitoes maddening. Next morning John set out at dawn to get help while we waited. I was tired, desperately tired. The body lay on the stretcher and I laid a handkerchief on his wounds, which the ants and flies were attacking. I took my map case from underneath his head and placed his hat over his head. His face was a terrible grey white. I felt weaker and weaker and by eleven o'clock could hardly sit upright.[6]

Then half an hour later Second Lieutenant Crowe returned with fourteen men and a party of Malay Home Guards. Mallows' body was transferred to a stretcher that had been brought out, while the Home Guards cut a direct path through 1,500 yards of jungle to the nearest track which took several hours. It was nearly dark when they met the track where two trucks were waiting for them. Martin and his patrol had been out for twenty-six hours.

Tom Mallows was a Barnardo's boy who had been placed in care aged 10. He had been a regular soldier with the Suffolk Regiment since 1947, having joined them in Palestine. Martin never forgot Tom or that fateful day. Sixty years after his death, he applied for the Elizabeth Cross for him and with the help of Barnardo's, he traced his foster family and presented it to them. Tom's close comrade Bernie Elmer remembered their final haunting conversation the night before: 'He was in my tent and was two down from my bed. The night before we'd been in the NAAFI and he said to me in all seriousness, "You know Bernie, I'm going to die tomorrow", and his words came true.'[7]

It was a sad ending to a highly successful few months and the last time that a soldier of the Suffolk Regiment would be killed in action on active service.

Despite the loss of Mallows, the bandit killed by 6 Platoon was later identified as Kong Har, who had taken over from Liew Kon Kim as commander of 4th Company, MRLA. He had joined the MPAJA in 1942 and had been a member of the Malayan Communist Party since 1943. He had even run the Kajang section of the MPAJA Old Comrades Association before going into hiding in 1949.

It had been a close-run thing too for Sergeant Smith of 6 Platoon who had been shot in the neck in the action against him: 'He started firing and suddenly I felt a pain in my neck. It started to sting and I thought he's shot me through the throat. I was determined to get Kong Har and I hit him first time.'[8] As with all actions, Har's bandit cap was 'souvenired' and his watch taken. Many years later Sergeant Smith presented them to the Regimental Museum.

On 28 December 1952, a memorial service was held at Cheras Road Military Cemetery to remember all those of the battalion who had fallen during the campaign. While wreaths were laid at their graves, RSM Duffy read out the names of the fallen.

The day of 2 January 1953 saw the final patrol being launched by 10 Platoon, 'D' Company under the command of Lieutenant Tony Catchpole. He had been out to lay an ambush on the edge of a rubber estate near Kajang. Two bandits appeared and the ambush was sprung, killing both of them.

This officially brought the final score of communist terrorists killed and captured to 196: a record that was never to be beaten by any British unit serving during the Emergency. Five days later the battalion handed over operational responsibility to the 1st Battalion, Somerset Light Infantry, who had been shadowing them for some weeks. As the battalion prepared to leave Malaya, all agreed that theirs was a job well done. They were leaving on a high, but many of the locals were sad to see them go.

Preparations then began in earnest for the journey home. Officers' mess linen and silver were packed and sent down to Singapore. The Colours of the 1st Battalion had already gone home some weeks before to be at the forthcoming Coronation Parade in London. Malaya had not been kind to the Colours, and being 104 years old, they had been returned to Singapore to be placed in cold storage as it was feared that any more exposure to the harsh climate would damage their already fragile silk beyond repair.

With a bounty given by a planter, many of 6 Platoon bought brand-new suitcases to take home their additional 'souvenirs' from Malaya. The lucky ones had a bandit cap and Private Ross, the man who had been responsible for adding battle honours to the battalion's vehicles and the painter of many platoon signs, was kept busy for the last few days painting their owners' names and addresses upon them.

For many though, it was their jungle hat that was the most highly-prized souvenir of their service. They had been fashioned and stitched into every conceivable style, with everything from can-openers to grenade pins tucked into the loops around the crown that were designed to hold foliage. A multitude of knotted jungle bootlaces were woven around it and held up its brim in every conceivable style from cowboy Stetson to 'Robin Hood'. It was a unique expression of individuality in a drab and colourless period of soldiering and many found ingenious places to spirit them home as souvenirs.

The Selangor Club and the regimental contractor both made handsome donations to the battalion upon its departure. Both were added to the fund for the Regimental War Memorial homes that were being built in Bury St Edmunds and would shortly be completed. In their lifetime, their residents included many veterans of the Malayan Emergency.

At the time of their departure, there was no doubt that the tide had turned against the terrorists in central Malaya. The bandits had already pulled back deep into the jungle and had drastically scaled back their random attack patterns. Their equipment and arms were poor and often defective in the attack due to prolonged exposure to jungle conditions, so by early 1953 the bandits had lost the initiative and they would never regain it.

Advances in the use of long-range patrols and Special Forces expanded greatly in the months following the battalion's departure and units were now on active operations in the primary jungle for weeks on end, being resupplied by air and being delivered and collected from the jungle by helicopter.

In writing later of the battalion's service in Malaya, Lieutenant Colonel Ian Wight noted the main reason behind their success and his pride in having commanded the battalion between 1948 and 1951:

> The spirit and character of the Suffolk soldier is exemplified in the words of our Brigade Commander: 'The tremendous enthusiasm, speed of action and determination to close with the enemy was the outstanding feature displayed by this battalion, and in many cases made all the difference between success and failure.' The two finest jobs in the British Army are to command a first-rate infantry battalion, or to command a first-rate platoon, preferably in operations. This was my luck![9]

With the band and drums leading, on 8 January 1953 the battalion marched through the streets of Kuala Lumpur past the Secretariat where the High Commissioner, General Sir Gerald Templer took the salute. Later Templer, accompanied by the sultan of Selangor, visited the railway station to see the battalion on its way. It was a personal though not officially public 'thank you' for their efforts in helping to turn the tide of the Emergency.

As the carriages pulled away, the men cheered but many were sad at their departure. They had done great work in the three and a half years that they had served there. They had routed and then eliminated the feared Kajang Gang and its leader, and had worked with the local population to make their lives better and to remove the intimidating threat of communism from their communities.

An article published in *The Times* in 1953 succinctly recorded their campaign and their achievements:

> They are coming home after three and a half years, with the finest record of any unit which has been engaged in that difficult, nerve-wracking and long-drawn-out campaign against the terrorists in the jungle. Theirs has been the patient,

seemingly interminable and often seemingly hopeless task of seeking out a stealthy enemy, who never fights a pitched battle, but strikes suddenly and ruthlessly at civilian and soldier alike, and retreats as swiftly. The fusillade or the single shot from close range in thick jungle, the grenade hurled from ambush, the terrorist descent on peaceful people – these are his methods, for his object is to break the force of law and disrupt a peaceful economy by so terrifying the civil population that the state will be paralysed. The jungle cloaks him, and failing that he can merge himself into the civil population, which is too frightened to betray him. The Suffolks, many of them boys of 19 and 20 from quiet English homes have had to find and destroy him in detail, learning to know the jungle as he knows it, and withstand an exhausting climate and a war of nerves – and at the same time they have to impress on a suspicious and frightened people that they had come as friends and protectors, and that they were going to win. All honour to them, as they seem to have succeeded not only in beating the terrorists. Judging by the accounts of the demonstrations on their departure, they have also won the confidence of the people and in Malaya that confidence is half the battle. Suffolk will greet them on their return with immense pride for these warriors, while England lives at peace the bonds between the English counties and their regiments have been close-drawn. So many homes are anxious – and when our own men return we must not forget the others who carry on the fight.[10]

Docking at Liverpool on 13 February 1953, the battalion came home after nine years of active service. It had not been home since they left Britain for D-Day in June 1944, but in the years between it had carved itself an illustrious reputation.

The towns of Ipswich, Sudbury and Bury St Edmunds held special parades conferring the freedom of their boroughs to the regiment in recognition of their service in Malaya and presented the battalion with silver bugles to commemorate their achievements there.

Their success in Malaya prompted the question to be asked why the regiment should not now be given 'Royal' status, making it the 'Royal Suffolk Regiment'. Several campaigns were mounted in the press of the day, yet the regiment itself, ever self-effacing and modest, saw no need to push for such a title; being 'plain old Suffolk' was perfectly good enough for them. Their achievements in Malaya spoke for themselves and the regiment needed no added lustre of a royal title.

Photographs taken behind the scenes of the filming of *Operation Malaya* in late 1952. The director David MacDonald, left, views the action, while behind the camera was the cinematographer Christopher Challis, who worked with notable directors Michael Powell and Emeric Pressburger on such epics as *The Small Back Room*, *The Red Shoes* and later *The Battle of the River Plate*.

Local girls who worked at the Galloway Club and Iban and Tamil trackers who served with the battalion doubled up as communist bandits for the filming. Here they rest in a reconstructed basha awaiting their participation in the next shot. In the foreground rests an antique captured bandit shotgun.

Bemused Iban trackers and a local rubber tapper await their call on set. For men who had never seen a camera, let alone a movie camera, it was all quite new. Ibans were known to be suspicious people.

(**Above**) The culmination of the movie: the capture of a bandit by men of 12 Platoon. After a hand-to-hand scrap with Sergeant Aldridge (standing right), the bandit is caught and brought in for arrest and later trial.

(**Opposite, above**) A travelling entertainments show came to visit 'B' Company at Kuala Kubu Bharu in 1952. Brian Reece, better known as 'P.C. 49', holds an EY rifle in the foreground while backed by three beauties from his London show. Private Ron Newlands crouches in the right foreground with his Bren, while others of 4 and 6 platoons crowd around behind. In the centre at the back is Ted Philips. Reece had performed many shows to British troops in the Far East and his hat was adorned with many badges and formation signs picked up on his travels.

(**Opposite, below**) Another Forces show, this time at Kajang. Here Donald Peers dances with a female compère watched by Bert Brownbill. After his performances, Brownbill took time to meet the men and offered to write to their parents at home to let them know that they were all well. Peers later caught a tropical disease which forced him to be hospitalized for several weeks, cancelling his planned London show, but once he was fit again he started off on another tour of British units serving in Korea.

Bert Brownbill and some of the entertainers pose with men of 5 Platoon and the Support Platoon. Standing left is the singer Lucille Graham who performed during the show and later signed photos for those who requested them.

A combined police and battalion patrol crosses a weir to head up into the plantations beyond Batu. By the end of their tour, such patrols were commonplace. The Malay Special Constables can be seen first and third in line, identified by their black berets.

204

(**Opposite, above**) In the months following the death of Sir Henry Gurney when his car was ambushed near Fraser's Hill, a close watch was kept on lonely and vulnerable stretches of road where potential ambushes could occur. Here a road watch of 7 Platoon, 'C' Company observes a planter's car speed by.

(**Opposite, below**) Fatigued from patrolling, Lieutenants Pat Hopper, left, and Richard Wilson, right, stop for a smoke with an Owen-gunner from their 3 Platoon patrol in late 1952. Richard would go on to become adjutant of both the 1st and 4th battalions of the regiment, overseeing the tricky task of amalgamation with the Royal Norfolk Regiment in 1959.

(**Above**) Lieutenant 'Bob' Godfrey drinks tea from his mess tin during a rest while patrolling a steep rubber plantation in the hills near Banting. The jungle appears to have already started to reclaim this land.

A pause under the thick, impenetrable jungle canopy for a small patrol of 5 Platoon. Here Private Wiggins, left, and Lance Corporal Atkins, right, are both armed with M2 carbines. Wiggins wears a camouflage face veil around his neck as a sweat rag. The cradle for the water bottle – modelled on American designs with two popper studs – can be seen on his right hip.

An Owen-gunner of 4 Platoon poses for a fellow comrade's camera under the piercing sunlight that has penetrated the thick jungle canopy above him. A lack of the Owen's magazine pouch suggests that this was not his personal weapon.

On the edge of a jungle clearing, Private Geoff Hobbs uses a No. 68 wireless set to make contact with base to arrange the patrol's collection. Geoff recalled that 'the poor signaller walked with a permanent stoop as a result of carrying the 68 set, and there was not an ounce of fat on him!'

KAJANG TERROR DIED ALONE
Suffolks fulfil their vow

He Killed The Terror Of Kajang

KONG HAR, the 36-year-old company commander of the Kajang Gang, died alone on Tuesday, his only companion a newly-recruited schoolboy. The rest of his gang fled before a Suffolks' charge.

The 1st Battalion Suffolks swore that they would get Kong Har before they left Malaya and for two months they had been searching the jungles for the successor of Liew Kon Kim. A "whisper" and a carefully planned operation led to Kong Har being shot dead three miles from Jendaram in the Telok Datoh district of Selangor.

For Maj. A. M. J. Dewar, the greying Company Commander of B Company of the 1st Suffolks, Kong Har's death is a satisfying end to his company's tour of duty in Malaya. One of his platoons was responsible for the death of Liew Kon Kim, the bearded terrorist chief of the Kajang Gang, who was succeeded by Kong Har. On Tuesday Maj. Dewar was leading the section which shot Kong Har.

The man who fired the first shot to disable Kong Har, who was worth $13,000, was Sgt. R. Smith, a regular, who with Maj. Dewar was leading 2 Section of 6 Platoon, as they pushed through thick jungle.

About 40 yards ahead they saw movement in the undergrowth. In a few seconds it became certain that it was about ten terrorists on the move.

"At the same time a Bren gun opened up in the rear and I remember somebody threw three grenades," said Sgt. Smith. "The rear men turned round to face the firing at the back and at the same moment Maj. Dewer shouted 'charge.'

"I felt something pull at my neck, I thought I had been hit but the bullet only knicked the skin. I looked ahead and there was a terrorist behind a tree with a carbine in his hand.

"I fired at him and he dropped."

Maj. Dewar also fired at the two terrorists in front while a Bren gunner sprayed the area. The rest of the section charged through the area but the other terrorists had made off. The man whom Sgt. Smith had hit was Kong Har.

"I think Kong Har tried to act as a rearguard for the rest while they rallied," said Maj. Dewar yesterday. "He fought hard and if we had

MAJOR DEWAR (centre), Officer Commanding, "B" Coy., Suffolk Regiment, and Second Lieutenant Hands, (right) now at a university in England, who killed Liew Kon Kim, Selangor's bearded terrorist leader, for which he was awarded the M.C.

Gang Left Leader To Die Alone

not charged he might have hurt us.

"As soon as I examined him I thought he might be Kong Har for I discovered he was carrying not only a carbine but a brand new pistol. He was also carrying five fountain pens in his pocket."

Lying next to Kong Har, killed in the Suffolks attack, was an 18-year-old youth also dressed in a terrorist uniform. He was the only man to stay with his leader. The rest scattered as the few leading men of the Suffolks' section charged.

The fleeing terrorists, leaving their leader behind, ran into a Suffolks ambush and cut back into the jungle. Two sections chased three of the terrorists at a steady run for 1,500 yards led by an Iban tracker. Three times they opened fire on the gang.

With them was a woman terrorist so heavily perfumed that the soldiers could almost follow the terrorists by their scent.

A terrorist Bren gunner dropped back and opened fire on the section killing one of the soldiers. Then the terrorists split and ran individually and the trails were lost.

Kong Har was another brutal terrorist, known throughout the Telok Datoh district. He had been trailed by the Suffolks for months and he was killed during a carefully planned operation which resulted in two other terrorists being killed.

"A" and "B" companies of the Suffolks and men from the Royal Artillery took part in the operation while guns laid down a barrage. A 3,000-yard wide area was enclosed while four patrols swept through. One of the patrols, led by Second-Lieut. P. Bird, a National Service Officer, saw two terrorists coming towards them. They let them come forward and then opened fire. Lieut. Bird killing one while L/Cpl. Harris killed the second terrorist.

This gave the Suffolks a total score for the day of four terrorists killed and one wounded although it is thought that others were wounded during the chase.

A report of the action in which was Kong Har was eliminated in November 1952. The image which was used was at least six months old and showed Second Lieutenant Ray Hands MC, who was then at home at university.

A Bren-gunner of 'D' Company is seen here in an elaborately constructed basha. As a form of identification, he wears a Suffolk Regiment cap badge on his hat, mounted on a yellow square of cloth. Just visible under the attap leaves, one sock can be seen hung up to dry.

(**Above**) The battalion's 3in mortars in action at Klang in October 1952. The bombs were primed in the back of the truck, inserted back into their cardboard tubes, then carried over to the weapon to be fired. Private Colin Smith, who served in the Mortar Platoon, reckoned that a good crew could get four bombs into the air before the first one landed!

(**Opposite, above**) Being wounded in the depths of the jungle presented a major logistical problem of how to evacuate a casualty to hospital as soon as possible. Here on Operation ASBAB, Corporal Toms of 'D' Company has the luxury of resting his sprained ankle for a few days in a jungle camp before being evacuated by helicopter. Note Corporal Aldridge's 'bumpers': the black and white hockey boots that men changed into after a hard day's patrolling.

(**Opposite, below**) For most of the day, this is what a soldier saw when trekking in file through the jungle. A patrol of 'C' Company moves on through the elephant grass into the thick jungle beyond. The soldier seen here carries his water bottle strapped onto the top of his small pack. Below his poncho is rolled with what appears to be a dry pair of grey woollen socks tucked inside. Packs were worn loose in this fashion, slung low on their straps ready to be ditched if chase had to be given.

Living up to their motto of 'Death from above', the Mortar Platoon in action in 1952. This was the last time that the mortars of the battalion were used in anger. In later postings in Germany and Cyprus, their use was restricted to training exercises only.

Two Dyak trackers of 'A' Company armed with No. 4 rifles pose for 'Tiger' Horton's camera. The tracker on the left holds the hilt of his parang knife in his left hand with a long length of human hair dangling from it. The tracker on the right carries a shorter knife or 'golok'.

Outside their quarters at Sungei Besi, Second Lieutenants Pat Bird and Martin Knowles pose in their newly-procured sarongs. Such local dress, although comfortable, was not encouraged! Pat also appears to have sourced a pair of locally-made sandals or 'chupplis'.

A self-portrait of Second Lieutenant Pat Bird taken using the mirror in his room. Pat commanded 6 Platoon for the second half of 1952 and was responsible for turning around their fortunes in the bandit-hunting stakes, and was later Mentioned in Dispatches. After university, Pat went on to work for Cadbury's before starting his own successful business.

Breakfast at Sungei Manggis for Second Lieutenant Martin Knowles. After going up to Cambridge, Martin worked for Royal Dutch Shell, being head of their lubricants marketing division. He returned several times to Malaysia on work and was feted by his Malaysian colleagues, who were 'always at pains to publicly express their gratitude for what the Suffolks had done to help ensure the independence of their country.'

In Malaya, the battalion used weapons that they were not to use anywhere else. Here, Lieutenant Richard Wilson photographed his M2 carbine alongside an Owen submachine gun outside his accommodation.

(**Above**) An important visit by the High Commissioner, General Sir Gerald Templer, to congratulate the officers of the battalion before their tour came to an end in January 1953. From left to right: Second Lieutenants Paul Taylor, Robin Farmer and Alexander Thomson, Lieutenants Bob Godfrey, Bernard Corner and Tony Cobbold, the High Commissioner, Lieutenant Colonel Philip Morcombe (back to camera), the GOC Malaya, Major General Sir Hugh Stockwell, Major Bertie Bevan and the Padre, the Reverend Hugh Robinson.

(**Opposite, above**) While resting at Penang, a chance to take 'official' photographs of many of the battalion's platoons. Here 9 Platoon is seen with their commander, the 'Chief Nutter' Lieutenant Horrex. Back row: Privates Charlie Dike, unknown, unknown, Bidwell, Baker, unknown, 'Spiv' Riseborough and Stacey. Middle row: Privates Bert Cook, Bert Hall, unknown, unknown and 'Fuzzy' Knights, Corporal 'Tangy' Lee, Privates Bob Mason, unknown, unknown, Regan and Butler. Front row: Lance Corporal Roper, Sergeants Dickson and Ron Evans, Lieutenant Alan Horrex, Major John Fisher-Hock ('C' Company commander), CSM 'Nanny' Keeble and Corporal 'Tommo' Thompson. The original 9 Platoon sign with the leaping 'nut' can be seen in front.

(**Opposite, below**) Right up until the very last few days of their tour, patrolling continued. A patrol of 'D' Company moves through the beluka on the edge of the Sepang Estate. The estate, which was owned by the London Asiatic Rubber and Produce Company Limited, gave the battalion a sizeable bounty upon their departure to thank them for their actions in protecting their property. It was given to the Regimental Memorial Homes Fund in February 1953.

Following the stream was often quicker than trying to hack through the jungle. Here a section of 4 Platoon, 'B' Company moves cautiously forward. In the centre, Lance Corporal Alex Knightly is seen pausing for a comrade to take a photograph. Knightly carries his pack slung over his shoulders, with a pair of plimsolls strapped to the loop on the back. Half a mess tin can be seen here too, held in place by its wire handle pushed through the loop.

Another view of the patrol moving along the stream. Private Denis Lewin at the back follows Lance Corporal Burch through the water. Lewin carries his No. 5 jungle carbine crooked over one arm held comfortably with a finger through the trigger guard for support. Often the sling was removed altogether, less it got caught on the foliage and undergrowth. The sling swivel was secured in place with a piece of tied bootlace to stop it clanking.

Form ORS/ZZ/1.

SECRET

OPERATION REPORT

1. Fill in appropriate parts of this form for every foot operation carried out by your unit or sub-unit. In the case of police it should be noted that this form is not required for routine police patrols or static guards.
2. A fresh form is required whenever the size of the patrol or party is changed or when an ambush is laid (e.g. a platoon going out on patrol, splitting into two small patrol parties, one of whom lays an ambush would submit :—
   (a) One form covering period of platoon patrol.
   (b) One form for each of the small patrol parties.
   (c) One form for the ambush).
3. Detailed instructions for filling in are given on the other side of this form.
4. When filled in the form will be sent to :—
   Director of Operations,
   Operational Research Section,
   Bluff Road,
   KUALA LUMPUR.
5. Higher formations will NOT delay or ask for copies of the completed form.

If your operation is a patrol state briefly the task.

To eliminate 2 Min-yuen seen on the Sungei Ramal Estate, Serdang.

Give month and date/time covered by this report.

From 1200 23 Sept to 1600 23 Sept

From to

Total Hours 4

Map reference of site of action or ambush

Patrol/Ambush party ordered out by :—

Name E T Lummis Rank Major Appointment OC D Coy. 1 Suffolk

If you have been in action attach a narrative and sketch showing bandit and own weapon position showing spacings in yds. Use foolscap for this and fasten it securely to this form.

Any additional information you want to give may be written in this space. This includes discovery of bandit camps, food dumps, stoppages to weapons, use of dogs, possible cause of failure of action etc.

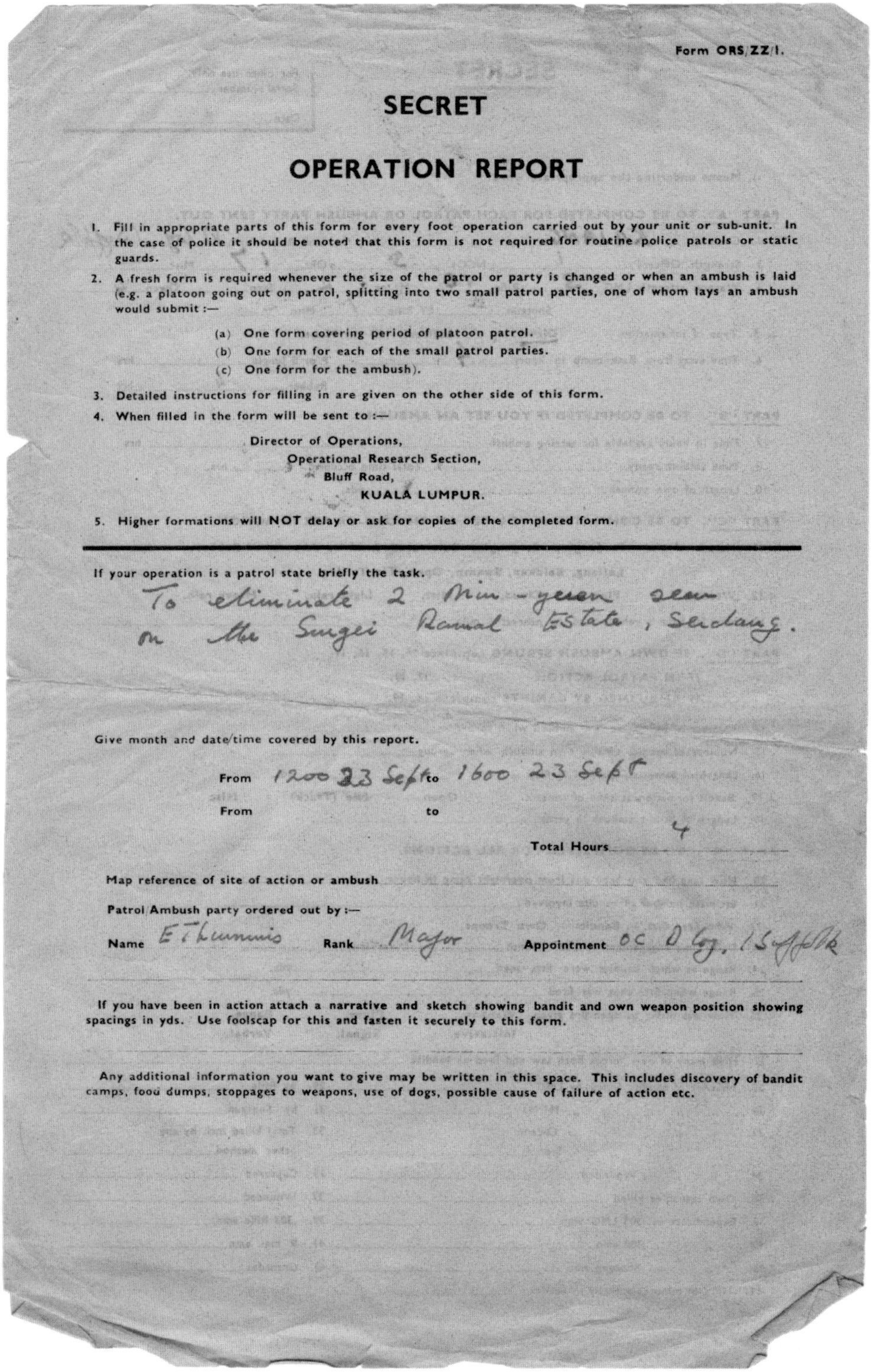

A secret action report complied by Second Lieutenant Robin Farmer after a patrol in Sungei Ramal Estate in September 1952. The reverse of the form gave space for details of weapons carried and the number of rounds expended in the action.

A patrol of 'A' Company crosses a swollen river. On such typical 'one-day ops' the men carried no packs, only arms and ammunition. These patrols were usually of four to six hours' duration and often involved a sweep into the jungle from an agreed spot and collection again from another a few hours later. The man in the foreground carries his Bren gun aloft to keep it out of the water. Behind him, Lance Corporal Len Spicer of the battalion Intelligence Section accompanies the patrol.

A patrol of 2 Platoon, 'A' Company stops two rubber tappers on their bicycles. Here as their papers are scrutinized, a Bren-gunner looks on. His Bren is supported by a wide webbing strap, salvaged from an air-drop pannier; its distinctive quick-release buckle can be seen on his right hip. Tappers were often the vital link between the bandits and their supplies of food and arms. Every conceivable place on a bicycle could hold a secret message requesting either, and each tapper had to be meticulously searched.

Tea in the ulu. On his last patrol with 'B' Company, Private Bernie Elmer asks a comrade to take one last picture of him in the centre with Private Gough left and Private Jackson right. Despite its unreliability, even at this late stage of operations, the older Sten gun was still being carried alongside the Owen. Within a fortnight, all three would be leaving Malaya, homeward bound for Liverpool.

'Not much more of this to go.' Privates Duff and Wyant outside their basha on a patrol in November 1952. Their shelter is two poncho capes snapped together and slung over a pole supported on a pair of 'Y'-shaped branches.

After bashas have been made, another crucial task often had to be performed. Here with the aid of a cigarette, Private Clark is removing leeches from Private Newbury's chest. Clark has already changed into hockey boots and blue PT shorts. In the foreground, a spoon, mug and mess tins can be seen hung on the basha's supporting stick.

(**Opposite, above**) Sharing a pack as a pillow, men of 'B' Company sleep wrapped up against the chill and the mosquitoes. Here with sleeves rolled down and one with his face wrapped in a towel, they will soon be woken for breakfast and to get ready to continue with the patrol for another day.

(**Opposite, below**) For Private 'Eddie' Burrows of 'C' Company being shot through the legs by a bandit on a patrol near Klang necessitated a stretcher to be made in the jungle from branches over which poncho capes were slung and held in place with rifle slings. The going was tough, carrying the wounded man out to the pick-up point, but after four hours they made it back to the road and he spent a 'pleasurable' six weeks in hospital in Singapore.

(**Above**) One of the last bandits to be eliminated by the battalion was on a 'D' Company patrol led by Lieutenant Catchpole. His body was secured to a branch using his own belt and he was carried out for identification. His body is seen later, slung across the wheel arches of the truck that came to collect the patrol.

A bandit is captured alive by a patrol of 11 Platoon, 'D' Company in October 1952. Here he sits on the ground, being closely guarded by the patrol. In the fading light, they await transport to send him to the police station for interrogation.

Members of 6 Platoon who participated in the Kong Har patrol. Their Platoon Commander, Second Lieutenant Pat Bird, can be seen second right.

THE PATROL of the 1st Suffolks, who killed Kong Har, the Kajang terrorist chief, and one of his men, on Tuesday.

'Peachey and the Bandit.' Once it was known that a bandit had been killed, the base party would bring up the collecting transport as close as possible to save men hours of heavy trudging with the corpse. Private Peachey, left, of the MT Detachment brings out a weapons carrier truck and helps to load the dead bandit aboard. A water bottle in its carrier has been draped over the front grille of the truck to cool water for the returning patrol.

The end of a long and tiring patrol. Here men of 1 Platoon, 'A' Company smile for the camera as they await their transport. Sitting left at the back is 'Tiger' Horton, while seated second right is Private Alf 'Pete' Peters. Pete was called up for National Service in 1948, but liked the army life so much that he signed on for a further five years' regular service. He later spent his working life with Dexion in Birmingham, famous the world over for their easy-to-assemble steel shelving.

(**Opposite, above**) 'My last patrol,' wrote Private Denis Lewin on the back of this photograph. Here a patrol of 4 Platoon, 'B' Company boards a truck back to Kajang. Lance Corporal Alex Knightly sits on the tailboard with cigarette in mouth, while the Iban tracker, closest to camera, passes up his pack. Several of those here wear the lightweight woollen pullover developed for the 1944 Pattern equipment. It can be identified by the reinforcing pads on the shoulder, through which the epaulette of the shirt passed. The Iban appears to wear a US-made 'Daisy Mae' fatigue cap rather than a British-made jungle hat. These were not uncommon in the very early days of campaigning when British equipment was in short supply.

(**Above**) A meeting of the army, the police, local chiefs and planters. In the informal surroundings of a café at Sungei Manggis, Second Lieutenant Pat Hopper in the centre eats his breakfast while the meeting takes place. Behind him, representatives from the Federation Police can be seen, with their distinctive khaki drill uniforms with black lanyards and dress embellishments. Another policeman sits on Pat's left, his 9mm Browning Hi-Power pistol visible in its leather holster.

(**Opposite, below**) A final photograph of members of 6 Platoon with their most prized possession: a captured bandit flag. A similar flag was captured by men of 11 Platoon, 'D' Company on a patrol in 29 April 1951. This flag can still be seen on display in the Suffolk Regiment Museum.

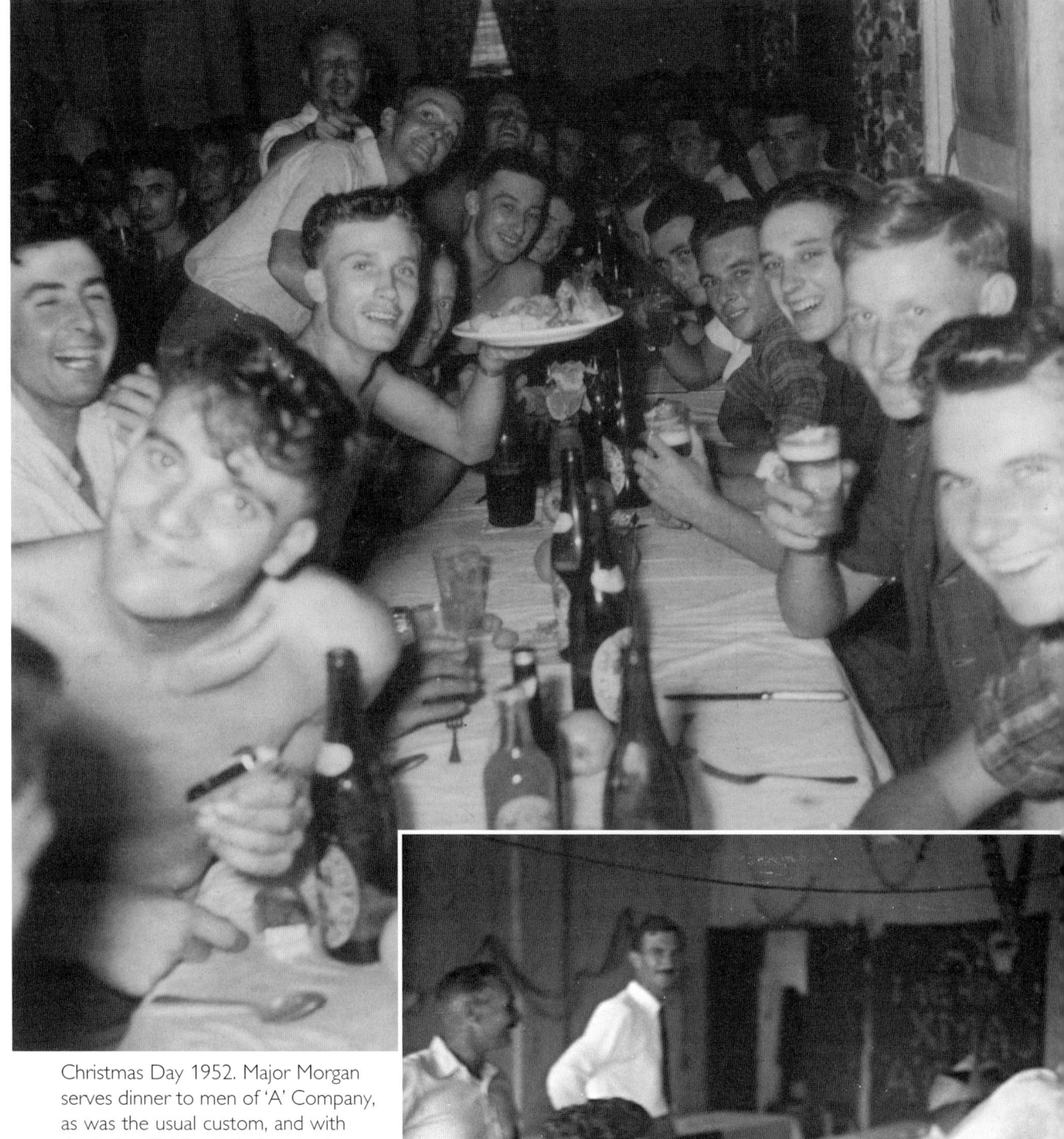

Christmas Day 1952. Major Morgan serves dinner to men of 'A' Company, as was the usual custom, and with the help of Major O'Reilley, he later distributes a free bottle of 'ABC' beer to each man.

The Support Company's Christmas party, 1952. Their company flag can be seen on the wall with their emblem of a stick man with a halo sitting on the letter 'S'. Each man received a free bottle of beer and an orange.

A patrol of 'B' Company pauses during a sweep of the Kuala Langat swamp. This was one of the higher areas of ground just out of the water.

Lance Corporal Tom Mallows, photographed while serving with the Support Company in early 1952. Tom was killed on patrol on 25 November 1952 in the Kuala Langat swamp.

A sombre scene. This photograph is believed to show men of 5 Platoon sitting solemnly with body of Lance Corporal Mallows covered in a groundsheet cape. Their disappointment and sadness is evident on their faces. Exhausted, they wait for the rescue party under Second Lieutenant Crowe to return. Tom was the last soldier of the Suffolk Regiment to be killed on active service.

The body of Lance Corporal Tom Mallows is laid to rest at Cheras Road Cemetery. Here, twenty men of the Suffolk Regiment now lie who died on active service during the Malayan Emergency. Their graves are still immaculately cared for today.

A special farewell for the Battalion, who were accorded the honour to march through the streets of the Malayan capital, Kuala Lumpur, as they started on the first leg of their journey home to the UK.

SUFFOLKS TO GET SPECIAL FAREWELL

KUALA LUMPUR, Friday.

KUALA LUMPUR is giving a special farewell to the 1st Battalion the Suffolk Regiment which is leaving for Britain after three and a half years of successes against the terrorists in Selangor.

With fixed bayonets, drums beating and colours flying, the victorious Suffolk Battalion, whose men have put out of action nearly 200 terrorists, will march through Kuala Lumpur on Thursday to board the train for the start of their journey.

This is the first farewell parade to be held in the Federal capital. It has been specially approved by the Sultan of Selangor.

The High Commissioner, General Sir Gerald Templer,

(**Above & opposite**) 'That there's some corner of a foreign field. That is forever Suffolk.' Before departing in January 1953, a service of commemoration was held at Cheras Road Cemetery where the battalion padre, the Reverend Hugh Robinson gave thanks for the lives of those who were buried there. From an altar of drums he took the service, after which wreaths were laid on the graves of all those of the regiment who were buried there. The battalion commander Lieutenant Colonel Morcombe gave a final salute before the battalion marched away.

First trouble spot: MALAYA

The Suffolks go for their 200th Red

Express Staff Reporter: Singapore, Sunday

THE fighting Suffolks of Malaya were out in the jungle today trying to find and kill their 200th Communist guerrilla before they sail for Britain on Thursday.

Their total up to this afternoon—198—is easily the biggest bag by any British unit.

Just short of their target for a double century, the Battalion had by the time they came home, eliminated 196 bandits: a record never beaten by any British unit serving there during the Emergency.

While their name was being lauded across Selangor, the battalion made its preparations to depart. Here Private 'Spiv' Riseborough of 9 Platoon, 'C' Company photographs his masterpiece of a Suffolk Regiment cap badge painted onto the side of his kitbag.

Ready to depart from Kuala Lumpur railway station, and a special farewell to Miss H.E.C. Butler, the battalion's very own WVS lady. She had been a great champion of the battalion during their time in Malaya, personally organizing for the band of 13/18 Royal Hussars to play at Minden Day in 1952. She organized countless other recreational and educational visits for the men of 1st Suffolk and when the battalion departed in January 1953, she was presented with a silver cigarette case as a token of appreciation for her assistance. Note the souvenir Suffolk Regiment cap badge on her handbag.

The official farewells over, the train pulls out of Kuala Lumpur station to much applause. As the band of the Queen's Own, Royal West Kent Regiment played the Malayan national tune of *Terang Bulan* (*Bright Moon*), Private George Flory, left, smiles at the thought of finally going home. As one reporter noted: 'It was a fitting farewell, for there is no doubt that the Fighting Suffolks will long remember their three and a half year sojourn in Malaya.'

Possibly the very last photograph taken of the battalion in Malaya. Second Lieutenant Richard Wilson captures the GOC Malaya, Major General Sir Hugh Stockwell, waving the battalion goodbye. As Richard later recalled: 'I had no idea if it would come out as I had to jump back on before the train left without me!'

'HELLUVA FINE JOB,' TEMPLER TELLS THE 1st SUFFOLKS

KUALA LUMPUR, Friday.

"YOU have done a helluva fine job," the High Commissioner, Gen. Sir Gerald Templer, told the 1st Battalion of the Suffolk Regiment today.

Five minutes later a breathless officer hurried up to tell Sir Gerald that one of their patrols had just reported on the field radio that they had killed one more of the Kajang gang.

The Suffolks—champion bandit killers among the British Battalions here—are making supreme last minute efforts to bring their score of terrorist eliminations to 200 before they leave the country next Thursday.

With today's kill, their score stands at 196 kills and captures—almost double that of any other British battalion.

At one Suffolk camp today Sir Gerald inspected men armed and equipped for another jungle patrol.

The same men had returned to camp at 4 a.m. today after an all-night search through swampy jungle.

Though in six days' time they will be finished with Malaya and its terrorists, the Suffolks are determined to get their 200th Communist.

Even the packing of kit for the journey is being neglected.

Sir Gerald today toured their company camps in the dual role of grateful High Commissioner and proud general.

I thank you

As High Commissioner, he told the men: "I want to thank you for all the magnificent work you have done on behalf of all the people of Malaya.

"I also want to pay tribute to all the people with whom you have worked—the district officials, the police, and so on, for without working hand in hand with them you could not have produced your results.

"There is a need for everyone out here to co-operate.

"Perhaps the reason for the difference in successes between units fighting here depends on the amount of co-operation they have with officials and the police and the public.

"Certainly your co-operation has been on a very high standard." he said.

"Some of you have seen what happens to a wretched rubber tapper who will not toe the Communist Party line. Remember it.

"We are fighting this evil out here today with bullets as we are fighting it in Korea and Indo-China.

"But if the shooting war stopped tomorrow we would still be fighting Communism. We are fighting it all over the world."

Three cheers

Speaking as a soldier, Sir Gerald said: "I do not like to make comparisons between units but as I have been quoted in newspapers as saying that Green Howards killed the most bandits I want to say to you that you have killed or eliminated twice as many terrorists as any other British battalion.

"You really have done a helluva fine job.

"Your regiment has a great history and since coming here you have added to that glorious history," he said.

"**One special thing you can be proud of is that you have never lost a weapon to the Communist terrorists.**"

The men gave him three cheers.

As he was moving off after his inspection of "A" and "D" companies, Sir Gerald's car was stopped by an officer who told him excitedly that news had just come through on the field radio that a patrol of "D" company had just made a kill. But it was not yet confirmed.

Sir Gerald was accompanied on his tour by the G.O.C., Malaya, Maj.-Gen. Sir Hugh Stockwell.

General Sir Gerald Templer's personal accolade to the men of the Battalion was much appreciated and much cherished by those who served in Malaya. This clipping was proudly posted home by Sergeant Gordon Broughton to his mother in Norwich.

Boarding MV *Georgic* at Singapore, the battalion was coming home after nine years abroad. With kitbags marked for Meeanee Barracks, Colchester, they have left behind their jungle webbing and No. 5 rifles in Malaya. Their brigadier, Brigadier Lambert, came to see them off and wrote later of their great achievements in Malaya: 'At no time has the Battalion ever failed or hesitated to attempt what was asked of them, and their keenness and enthusiasm have been an inspiration to all.' Their journey home took almost a month.

Daily Sketch, Thursday, January 8, 1953

They wore 30,000 boots

THE bandit-hunting Suffolks, who have worn out 15,000 pairs of boots in three years of Malayan jungle patrols, sail for home from Singapore to-day.

The Suffolks, the First Battalion of the Suffolk Regiment, killed 180 bandits and captured 13.

This is nearly double that of any other British battalion. They lost 12 killed and 24 wounded. General Sir Gerald Templer, High Commissioner in Malaya, thanked them in his farewell address for the "magnificent work you have done in the fight against international Communism."

The battalion's booty included 20 carbines, 68 rifles, 34 pistols, 23 shotguns, 56 grenades, nearly 6,000 rounds of ammunition, seven Bren gun magazines and four bombs.

THEY BEAT RED TERRORISTS

Men of the First Battalion, Suffolk Regiment, are on their way back to England with the best record yet of any United Kingdom unit which has served in the campaign against Malaya's Communist terrorists.

They have killed or captured more terrorists than any other United Kingdom battalion, and nearly as many as each of two Gurkha battalions which have been stationed longer in Malaya. Their victims have included more top-flight Communists than those of any other unit.

At the same time, the Suffolks, who left Kuala Lumpur on the first stage of their journey on January 9, have become Malaya's most decorated battalion. Their awards include two DSOs, nine MCs, one MBE, one DCM, one MM and one BEM.

During their service in Malaya, the Suffolks have spent most of their time in Southern Selangor, the state in which Malaya's capital, Kuala Lumpur, is situated. There they have carried on a personal vendetta with the Kajang "Killer Gang," one of the most bloodthirsty bands of terrorists in Malaya.

While some of the gang remain, their ranks have been broken and their leadership decimated by the patient, persistent Suffolks.—Reuter.

The price of their success. During the Battalion's tour over 15,000 pairs of the flimsy canvas and rubber jungle boots were worn out. It was later calculated that combined, men of the Battalion walked over a million miles during their tour in Malaya.

Chapter Six

The Fight Continues

After the battalion left Malaya, many of its pioneering actions became widely adopted. The battalion's work in destroying the heartland of the communist infrastructure around the capital city of Kuala Lumpur did much to shatter the morale of the terrorists and pushed them further north into deep jungle.

The supply of long-range patrols by air now became commonplace, while the importance of using native guides on operations was greatly expanded upon. The Iban Platoon, which was pioneered by the battalion, was later reorganized and re-formed into a dedicated regiment named the 'Sarawak Rangers'.

The Special Air Service, disbanded after the war, was reborn in 1951 into the 'Malayan Scouts' and the following year it became 22 SAS Regiment. Now they developed their role in counter-insurgency operations, expanding on the techniques used during the war by their leader, former Chindit Brigadier 'Mad Mike' Calvert, to establish elaborate and highly-fortified positions deep in the jungle from where they could strike out on operations.

These positions would be resupplied from the air, with virtually no opposition from the terrorists. These operations proved successful and by the end of 1954, it was recorded that 723 terrorists had been killed that year from a remaining enemy force of around 3,000. This force also pioneered the use of parachuting troops into primary jungle.

By April 1955, large areas of Malaya, most notably in the east in Pahang, Terengganu and Northern Johore, had been declared 'White' and free of communist influence. It was therefore felt by the High Commissioner, in keeping with the planned progression to independence, that a general election could be held in these areas.

At the insistence of General Templer, every Malay citizen was given the right to vote, including the Chinese. Now, as Lieutenant General Sir Brian Horrocks noted, when they had a 'stake in the franchise'[1] they finally felt that they belonged to a nation and could play a part in its administration. Soon any feelings of sympathy with the communists still at large in the jungle rapidly decreased.

An important factor in turning the population against the terrorists was the bringing to trial of captured personnel. It was often questioned as to whether the cost justified the end, but by showing that justice was being delivered in a lawful manner according to the laws of the country, it gave faith to the Malays and the Chinese that terrorists would be brought to book and if found guilty they would be sentenced. Some senior military personnel argued that the cost of trial and judicial representation could be saved with the cost of a sixpenny bullet in the jungle, but those crucial 'hearts and minds' that General Templer advocated winning could never be won by such acts.

The rebirth in September 1955 of the 28th (Commonwealth) Brigade which had served in the Korean War now brought numerous units from Australia, New Zealand and Rhodesia to assist in operations, giving a new impetus to the campaign.

By July 1957 almost 60 per cent of Malaya had been declared free from terrorist interference and as planned on 31 August, Malaya achieved its independence from Great Britain. Though many thought that this would be the end of the troubles, Commonwealth units remained there for a further three years, during which time a further 280 terrorists surrendered.

Peace talks with Chin Peng, the leader of the Malayan Communist Party, failed in 1958 and it was now clear that the terrorists' cause was lost. That year too, the states of Perak and Johore were declared 'White' and by July 1960, the restrictions that had been put in place twelve years earlier were finally repealed, except in a handful of areas in the north along the Thai border where Peng was now in hiding. He would remain there until his death in 2013.

There were lessons learned in Malaya that could have prevented others fighting costly insurgent wars in the Far East, but unlike the French in Indo-China and later the Americans in Vietnam, the campaign in Malaya was different.

Although parallels have been drawn between these conflicts and the Malayan Emergency, there were major differences between them. The Malayan Communist Party received virtually no support from outside Malaya, nor did it have a land border with a fellow communist country such as between Vietnam and China. The forces involved were minimal compared to those in Vietnam. Communist terrorists in Malaya numbered just 5,800 strong in comparison with a combined North Vietnamese Army (NVA) and Vietcong guerrilla force in excess of 250,000.

In Indo-China the French military leaders were so supremely confident of the inferiority of their enemy, the Viet Minh, and the superiority of their own men and firepower they were convinced that that alone would be enough to win the day. However, the underestimation of their enemy led to a costly and embarrassing defeat for the French at Dien Bien Phu in 1954.

In Malaya, however, the British were only too aware of the skill and cunning of their enemy and knew from the outset that they would need to change their tactics and operational doctrines, to fight their enemies as equals in their own territory deep in the jungle.

In Malaya, the civil powers cultivated and exploited an effective intelligence war, with the results being successful and swift. They saw the importance of keeping the

Malay people, the predominate race, happy as it was they who fought on loyally with the British deep in the jungle during the war.

The Malayan Emergency was to many young soldiers a unique, sometimes surreal and at times mentally difficult period in their lives, but the friendships that these young men forged here, far from home, have survived to this day. Many of the men who served here felt that the campaign was 'forgotten' and that it was greatly overshadowed by the Korean War. Perhaps now, this book will go some way to ensuring that this is no longer the case.

As a Suffolk National Serviceman, Pat Bird once said it was 'a terrific experience that I did not much like at the time, but which in retrospect, I would not have missed for the world.'[2]

Old soldiers never die. Here Len Spicer and Tony Coote pose on Minden Day with the tools of their trade fifty-five years earlier. Both men still retained their original jungle hats issued to them in Malaya.

Deep in conversation reliving old times. Kevin Duffy, the regimental sergeant major in Malaya, still with his famous handlebar moustache, chats with a Malaya veteran on Minden Day. Duffy travelled to Suffolk every year from his home in Cornwall to attend the reunion.

A march past of the Malaya veterans of the Hemel Hempstead Branch of the Old Comrades Association, Minden Day 2008. Seen here are many of those mentioned in this book: Hugh Doran, Dennis Levitt, Richard Scott (who travelled from Canada), Alex Knightly, 'Boz' Bostock (who travelled from Cape Town), Jim Hurst and Ray Burwood.

Happy days at John Blench's barbeque. Hugh Doran of 4 Platoon looks on bemused at members of 5 Platoon who assemble for a group photograph. Bernie Elmer, second left, Keith Garner and Fred Mullinder, second right, were called up together and remained close friends after leaving the regiment in 1953.

The best dressed man at any regimental function was Dick May with his regimental red and yellow silk shirt. Dick visited Malaya many times in his retirement and had this shirt 'run up' in Kajang when they visited in 2005. Along with his wife Jackie, they were huge supporters of the Old Comrades Association and later the 'Friends of The Suffolk Regiment'.

The Three Musketeers – Second Lieutenants Martin Knowles, Pat Bird and the late Robin Farmer – photographed at a Malaya veterans' luncheon in 2008. All three were contemporaries in Malaya and later Trieste, and all kept in contact with each other after they left the regiment.

The man who saved the Suffolk Regiment. Tony Rogers did much to ensure that the regiment's part in the Malayan Emergency would not be forgotten. He was an ardent chronicler of regimental life and produced the newsletters for the Hemel Hempstead Branch of the Old Comrades Association. At regimental functions, he could often be seen with a camera in hand recording the event for those who could not attend. He said proudly to the author one day that 'I'm like a stick of rock. Break me in half and you find the Suffolk Regiment running right through me from top to toe.'

The author with Bernie Elmer at John Blench's barbeque in July 2009. The 5 Platoon sign had been specially recreated for the event, where eight former members of the platoon were present.

A nation's award for campaigning during the Emergency: the General Service Medal with the Malaya Clasp. All the men of 1st Suffolk who served there between 18 July 1949 and 8 January 1953 were eligible for the award, and many wore it with pride in later years.

Notes

Chapter 1: Origins of the Emergency
1. 'The Peace Keepers' television interview with Peter Lilley, 1967.

Chapter 2: Acclimatization and Evolution
1. Interview with the author, Great Yarmouth, 2007.
2. Suffolk Regiment Old Comrades Association, Hemel Hempstead Branch Newsletter, September 2005.
3. Wight, Brigadier I.L., DSO, OBE, *Reflections of a Battalion Commander in Malaya*, Private, c.1988.
4. Interview with the author, Great Yarmouth, December 2009.
5. Interview with the author, Bury St Edmunds, March 2012.
6. Bird, P.B., *Personal Memoirs*, c.2000.
7. Email to the author, May 2014.
8. Farmer, R.L., *Personal Memoirs*, c.2008.
9. Suffolk Regiment Old Comrades Association, Hemel Hempstead Branch Newsletter, September 2008.
10. Interview with the author, Ipswich, May 2015.
11. Interview with the author, Diss, April 2012.
12. Suffolk Regiment Old Comrades Association, Hemel Hempstead Branch Newsletter, September 2008.
13. Interview with the author, Ipswich, May 2015.
14. Ibid.
15. Farmer, R.L., *Personal Memoirs*, c.2008.
16. Ibid.
17. Interview with the author, Diss, April 2012.
18. 'Campaigning in Malaya', *The Times*, May 1952.
19. Interview with the author, Great Yarmouth, December 2009.
20. Ibid.
21. Letter to the author, September 2020.
22. Letter to the author, August 2010.
23. Farmer, R.L., *Personal Memoirs*, c.2008.
24. Interview with the author, Ipswich, May 2015.

Chapter 3: The Upper Hand
1. 'The Suffolks are winning through more trouble', *Suffolk Chronicle and Mercury*, 21 April 1950.
2. Letter to the author, August 2010.
3. Coote, A.J., *National Service in Malaya 1951–53*, Private, February 1994.
4. Wight, Brigadier I.L., DSO, OBE, *Reflections of a Battalion Commander in Malaya*, Private, c.1988.
5. Farmer, R.L., *Personal Memoirs*, c.2008.
6. Coote, A.J., *National Service in Malaya 1951–53*, Private, February 1994.

7. 'The Peace Keepers' television interview with Sir Brian Horrocks, 1967.
8. Bird, P.B., *Personal Memoirs*, c.2000.
9. Ibid.
10. Suffolk Regiment Old Comrades Association, Hemel Hempstead Branch Newsletter, June 2005.
11. 'Campaigning in Malaya', *The Times*, May 1952.
12. Letter to Colonel W.N. Nicholson, 19 August 1953.

Chapter 4: 'The Best in Their Field'

1. Suffolk Regiment Old Comrades Association, Hemel Hempstead Branch Newsletter, June 2007.
2. Godfrey, F.A., *History of the Suffolk Regiment, 1946–1959*, Leo Cooper, 1988.
3. *Suffolk Regimental Gazette*, No. 499, First Quarter 1952.
4. *The Times*, March 1952 (exact date unknown).
5. Reproduced in *Singapore Standard*, 24 May 1952.
6. Reade, Major D.H. de T., 'Exploits of the Suffolk Regiment in Malaya', *Legion Magazine*, May 1952.
7. Godfrey, F.A., *History of the Suffolk Regiment, 1946–1959*, Leo Cooper, 1988.
8. 'An operation in Malaya', *Suffolk Regimental Gazette*, No. 501, Third Quarter 1952.
9. Coote, A.J., *National Service in Malaya 1951–53*, Private, February 1994.
10. 'Empire Warriors' television interview, 2004.
11. 'The End of the Bearded Wonder', *The Planter*, July 1952.
12. Suffolk Regiment Old Comrades Association, Hemel Hempstead Branch Newsletter, March 2008.
13. Suffolk Regiment Old Comrades Association, Hemel Hempstead Branch, 'The Suffolk Regiment: The story of the regiment told by the men who served', Private, 2004.
14. Wight, Brigadier I.L., DSO, OBE, *Reflections of a Battalion Commander in Malaya*, Private, c.1988.
15. Bird, P.B., *Personal Memoirs*, c.2000.
16. Ibid.
17. Ibid.
18. Ibid.
19. Private letter, 28 August 1951.
20. 'Bandit has outlawed Suffolks', *Malay Straits Times*, 24 July 1951.
21. 'NS men were terrific', *East Anglian Daily Times*, January 1953.

Chapter 5: The Race for 200

1. Private letter, 19 July 1952.
2. Fenney, Derrick, *Malay Mail*, 25 November 1952.
3. Suffolk Regiment Old Comrades Association, Hemel Hempstead Branch Newsletter, June 2006.
4. Ibid.
5. Ibid.
6. Ibid.
7. Interview with the author, Great Yarmouth, December 2009.
8. 'Suffolks fulfil their vow', newspaper clipping from collection of P.B. Bird (believed to be from the *Malay Mail*, July 1952).
9. Wight, Brigadier I.L., DSO, OBE, *Reflections of a Battalion Commander in Malaya*, Private, c.1988.
10. *The Times*, 10 January 1953.

Chapter 6: The Fight Continues

1. 'The Peace Keepers' television interview with Peter Lilley, 1967.
2. 'NS men were terrific', *East Anglian Daily Times*, January 1953.